Ah Hah!

The Inquiry Process of Generating
and Testing Knowledge

This book is part of the Goodyear Series in Education, Theodore W. Hipple, Editor, University of Florida

Other Goodyear Books in General Methods & Centers

A CALENDAR OF HOME/SCHOOL ACTIVITIES
JoAnne Patricia Brosnahan and Barbara Walters Milne

CHANGE FOR CHILDREN Ideas and Activities for Individualizing Learning
Sandra N. Kaplan, Jo Ann B. Kaplan, Sheila K. Madsen, Bette K. Taylor

CREATING A LEARNING ENVIRONMENT A Learning Center Handbook
Ethel Breyfogle, Susan Nelson, Carol Pitts, Pamela Santich

THE LEARNING CENTER BOOK An Integrated Approach
Tom Davidson, Phyllis Fountain, Rachel Grogan, Verl Short, Judy Steely, Katherine Freeman

ONE AT A TIME ALL AT ONCE The Creative Teacher's Guide to Individualized Instruction Without Anarchy
Jack E. Blackburn and W. Conrad Powell

OPEN SESAME A Primer in Open Education
Evelyn M. Carswell and Darrell L. Roubinek

THE OTHER SIDE OF THE REPORT CARD A How-to-Do-It Program for Affective Education
Larry Chase

THE TEACHER'S CHOICE
Sandra N. Kaplan, Sheila K. Madsen, Bette T. Gould

TEACHING FOR LEARNING Applying Educational Psychology in the Classroom
Myron H. Dembo

TRANSPERSONAL EDUCATION
Alton Harrison and Diann Musial

WILL THE REAL TEACHER PLEASE STAND UP? A Primer in Humanistic Education, 2nd edition
Mary Greer and Bonnie Rubinstein

A YOUNG CHILD EXPERIENCES Activities for Teaching and Learning
Sandra N. Kaplan, Jo Ann B. Kaplan, Sheila K. Madsen, Bette T. Gould

For information about these, or Goodyear books in Language Arts, Reading, Science, Math, and Social Studies, write to:
Janet Jackson
Goodyear Publishing Company
1640 Fifth Street
Santa Monica, CA 90401
(213) 393-6731

Ah Hah!

The Inquiry Process of Generating and Testing Knowledge

John A. McCollum
Southern Oregon State College

Goodyear Publishing Company, Inc.
Santa Monica, California

Library of Congress Cataloging in Publication Data
McCollum, John A.
  "Ah hah!"
  1. Learning, Psychology of. 2. Inquiry (Theory of knowledge) 3. Language arts. 4. Teachers,
Training of. I. Title
LB1051.M155   370.15'2   77-17137
ISBN 0-87620-053-6
ISBN 0-87620-052-8 pbk.

Copyright © 1978 by
Goodyear Publishing Company, Inc.
Santa Monica, California 90401

ISBN: 0-87620-053-6 (C)
       0-87620-052-8 (P)

Y-0536-6 (C)
Y-0528-3 (P)

Current printing (last digit)
10 9 8 7 6 5 4 3 2 1

Book produced by Ken Burke & Associates

Project editor: Judith Fillmore
Copyeditor: Sarah Betty Berenson
Text and cover designer: Christy Butterfield
Illustrator: Barbara Hack
Compositor: Publications Services

Printed in the United States of America

To Helen

Preface

All of us have experienced that exciting, stimulating moment when the puzzle fits together, the solution to the problem becomes evident, or we discover how "it" works—that moment when we suddenly see relationships that simply weren't evident before. There's a flash of insight, and we exclaim, "Ah hah!—I get it! That's how—or why—or how come!"

There is a big difference between acquiring the answer through that process and having someone tell us. We may find the answer someone else tells us to be interesting, but, generally, there isn't that feeling of success as when we "discover" it for ourselves through the process of personal inquiry.

The purpose of this book is to provide you with the necessary understandings and skills to implement the process of inquiry in your classroom. The word *inquiry*, as presented here, signifies that intellectual process by which people, when confronted with a problem, puzzling phenomenon, or discrepancy for which they cannot immediately account, generate and test ideas they find personally useful to explain the phenomenon and to predict consequences of similar circumstances. It is that process whereby learners develop meaning for themselves, as opposed to being *told* what is true, or right, or good. Inquiry is that natural learning process one sees when a tiny infant reaches out to grasp and examine an object. It occurs naturally and spontaneously throughout children's early life when they continue to generate personal meanings by exploring, testing, building, and asking innumerable questions preceded by *why* in an attempt to account for the tremendous array of puzzling phenomena that surround them. It continues to be observable in those instances beyond the beginning of school when children are provided the opportunity (or *take* the opportunity, sometimes against the wishes of teachers and parents) to confront puzzles that are personally relevant and to generate solutions that have personal meaning.

In this sense, inquiry is not something that must be *taught*, but, on the other hand, it doesn't necessarily just happen. It's not a question of whether or not it can or will occur, because obviously it does. The question is, Does it occur as a process of learning in the classroom? Although inquiry is a natural process of learning, it can very easily be inhibited or even prevented from happening. If it is to occur, certain conditions must exist. If the teacher is unaware of what those conditions are and the necessary strategies to establish and nurture them, inquiry will not likely be evident. That's what this book is about. It's designed to provide you with the knowledge and specific skills to implement the process of inquiry in the classroom.

The book is divided into five separate and distinct units of instruction preceded by an introductory chapter that relates inquiry to other learning processes. Each chapter presents knowledge and skills that help you understand and implement teaching and learning processes. Also, each chapter builds sequentially and developmentally on the previous to present and refine the knowledge and skills necessary to implement the inquiry process.

Chapter 1: Inquiry in Perspective

As you might expect, I have a strong bias in favor of inquiry as an important and useful learning process for students. However, of course, I am aware that it is not the only process nor necessarily the best for all learning situations. I have attempted in the first chapter, while building a rationale for more inquiry to occur in more classrooms, to also place it in perspective with other teaching and learning processes.

Chapter 2: Tuning In on Language

The teaching strategies necessary for the effective implementation of the inquiry process, while planned by the teacher in advance of a lesson, must be conducted in response to cues in the students' responses. This requires a sensitivity to the personal meaning that students have for the verbal symbols they use. Chapter 2 is designed to introduce you to the semantic structure of language and the skills necessary to tune in on the language of the classroom.

Chapter 3: Language Actions

The intellectual process going on inside a student's head can only be identified by the language she or he speaks or writes. And yet, most taxonomies for classifying cognitive processes are too cumbersome for teachers to use for immediately identifying the intellectual process in a student's response. This chapter presents a unique system for classifying cognitive processes. The system is easily learned and is highly effective in the implementation of the inquiry process. Chapter 3 helps you develop the skill to use this classification system.

Chapter 4: Interpreting

One of the easiest ways of seeing and understanding the process of inquiry is in relation to literature. A good writer does not tell you the main idea and then proceed to build a case to support it. On the contrary, a series of incidents, often conflict situations, are presented, which allow the reader to generalize personal interpretations. The author may lead the reader quite systematically toward a particular conclusion, but the generalization is always made by the reader, never by the author. Chapter 4 presents the theoretical background and specific teaching strategies for conducting the inquiry process in all content areas. Also, at the conclusion of the chapter, you are asked to conduct a teaching experience in which students interpret and test personal meanings.

Chapter 5: Fact or Fantasy?

The effectiveness of an idea is contingent on the degree to which it can be used to explain new situations or predict situations of similar circumstances. Chapter 5 is designed to develop teaching strategies that facilitate students testing for themselves the validity and reliability of ideas. Considerable emphasis is placed on the need for both the students and the teacher to be aware of the degree to which the instructional materials being used present either fact or fiction. Many teachers treat textbook content as factual when, in fact, it is often interpretations of interpretations of interpretations.

At the conclusion of this chapter, you will be asked to demonstrate your understanding of and skill in implementing the process of inquiry by designing and conducting a lesson that results in students analyzing a body of information, verbalizing personal interpretations (explanations of causal relationships), and testing interpretations for validity and/or reliability.

Chapter 6: Designing Curriculum for Inquiry Teaching

Inquiry is a learning process that can and should occur naturally and spontaneously many times during each day in the classroom. At the same time, however, each teacher has a major responsibility for designing and presenting a *planned* program of studies. If inquiry is to be an important and integral part of each student's experience in school, then the process must be an important and integral part of the planned curriculum. Chapter 6 presents a model for designing curriculum sequences that have as their basic learning method the inquiry process.

General Semantics

It is probably clear at this point that a fundamental goal is to help you develop a practical acquaintance with some principles and techniques of general semantics. Effective implementation of the inquiry process depends on teachers being highly sensitive to what students say and what they mean by what they say. Besides the obvious reason—that education itself is largely a symbolizing process of expressing and perceiving ideas in verbal form—there are at least two additional reasons why the teacher of the inquiry process must be aware of semantic principles and especially attentive to language behavior.

First, the teacher must realize that the meaning of anything a student says is a personal meaning. A teaching strategy that takes its cues from what the students are saying, rather than what the teacher is saying, requires the teacher to be highly sensitive to students' language and skillful in employing techniques to tune in on the personal meaning that students have for the words they use (see Chapter 2).

Second, the teacher must be a careful and expert listener because the only way the intellectual processes going on in the student's head can be inferred is from the words he or she is using. Again, words are symbols that represent personal meaning, and by analyzing the student's words it is possible to determine if she or he is recalling specific information, or theorizing, or interpreting, or whatever other processes psychologists and educators identify as occurring when a person is engaged in interacting with her or his world (see Chapter 3).

Humanizing Instruction

Another fundamental goal is to help you acquire the understandings and skills to employ a set of teaching behaviors that cause students to generate for *themselves* explanations of why things happen as they do. Part of this teaching strategy is based on learning how to design, sequence, and ask certain kinds of questions. But a very large part of it is based on being open, accepting, and respectful of the student. One of the simplest and yet most difficult of the teaching behaviors to employ (apparently since most of us have experienced so little of it in our own background of formal education) is the strategy of *not* judging the validity, reliability, or value of a student's explanations, but helping him or her to test the usefulness of his or her own ideas. To do so effectively requires the establishment of a humanistic and supportive teaching and learning relationship (see Chapters 4 and 5).

Format

The book is based on the assumption that most participants will proceed through the material as a member of a group, either in a college class or as a member of an in-service project. Since I believe that people need people in order to learn most effectively, I have included exercises and activities to be completed by each participant and then shared with other individuals to refine understandings and skills. Although it is entirely possible, and valuable, for you to proceed through the book independently, I am convinced that you will acquire a greater depth of understanding and skill if you share the products of each exercise and activity with interested colleagues.

When proceeding through some sections, you may feel uncomfortable in learning inquiry through materials that are expository or programmed in nature. However, the purpose of such exercises is to provide you with a base of information and a means of refining specific skills. The personal meaning of inquiry and the ability to implement inquiry strategies will occur as a result of generating ideas and skills for yourself and testing them in laboratory teaching activities. It is my sincere hope that you will find this to be an enjoyable, stimulating, valuable experience.

John A. McCollum

Acknowledgments

There are a number of individuals to whom I owe much for their assistance in the development of this book. I wish to express special acknowledgment to Fred Newton, Jeanne Butman, Sue Miller, and Keith Acheson. The germinal point for many of the ideas for this self-learning program occurred when we were all engaged in the initial phases of designing a teacher education program to integrate the work of Hilda Taba, J. Richard Suchman, and James Gallagher. I owe much to a great number of people who helped me crystallize those ideas: Katherine Aguon and Bob Peryon who were willing to try the ideas in their infancy and collect formative data; the teaching staff of schools in Ashland, Oregon, for allowing participants to try the activities in their classrooms; administrators and teaching colleagues at Southern Oregon State College, the University of Guam, the Northwest Regional Educational Laboratory, and the Ashland public schools for their support and assistance; and, especially, all those students at Southern Oregon State College and the University of Guam who gave extra time and effort to provide me with the necessary data to test, revise, and refine the strategies.

Special appreciation is given to Robert Devoe, who not only edited materials but also, because of his understanding of general semantics and teaching processes, contributed significantly to the content of the book.

Also, a very special thanks to Nancy Ellis who typed and retyped my often illegible original manuscript. Her beautiful personality helped make the project a very enjoyable experience.

J.M.

Contents

Ah Hah!

The Inquiry Process of Generating
and Testing Knowledge

1 Inquiry in Perspective

Overview

The necessity of developing the skill of self-generative learning in each learner grows more obvious and urgent every day. The incredible and accelerating explosion of knowledge, coupled with the frighteningly complex social, political, and economic problems of our contemporary era, demands an educational process that produces active, autonomous, self-generative learners. Productive individuals in the contemporary world *must* have the emotional stability to confront continuous change and the necessary skills to engage in a continuous process of personal problem solving.

Unfortunately, the educational process found in many classrooms does not contribute significantly to the development of this type of individual. On the contrary, it produces learners conditioned to seek someone else's answer, to ask, "What does the *authority* say?" rather than, "What is the problem and how might *I* solve it?" The predominant educational process in many classrooms encourages learners to avoid the responsibility of their own ideas—to distrust or ignore their own capacity for finding, creating, and testing meaning in the world. The process is often characterized by such teacher language as, "I'm not interested in what you think. Tell me what the book says."

Herbert Thelen[1] points out that the basic human experience is one of dealing with *conflict:* "Conflict between our wishes and the wishes of others, between our present needs and our future capabilities, between our animal nature and our social ethics, between what we are and what we want to be, between our easy habits and our creative urges." He feels it is unfortunate that conflict has become a dirty word, because it is through conflict that growth and education occur. People engage in problem solving or "conflict resolution" through two basic and natural processes: one is automatic and reflexive—involving such responses as attack, run, or freeze; the other is *inquiry*—involving such processes as insight or learning, such conscious methods as diagnosis, speculation, and hypothesis testing. This instructional program is about the process of inquiry—the method that gives students the opportunity to confront problems and to generate and test ideas for themselves.

What Is Inquiry?

One way to understand how the inquiry process functions is to examine it in perspective to other teaching-learning processes. Edwin Fenton[2] has suggested that a useful way of examining teaching strategies is to consider them as a continuum:

TEACHING CONTINUUM

EXPOSITION	DISCOVERY
(ALL CUES GIVEN)	(NO CUES GIVEN)

At one end of the continuum, the teacher and the textbook are authorities. The teacher tells the students what they shall learn and how they shall learn. The teacher states a generalization and provides the data that make it "true" (according to his or her and the textbook author's interpretation). At the other end of the continuum is the nondirective approach which allows students to discover meaning for themselves. The teacher will provide stimulus in the form of a problem and/or material, but the students are given complete autonomy to search and discover meaning for themselves.

Between these two extremes we can identify and place on the continuum other styles or types of teaching. Obviously, each teacher is unique. Each has his or her own set of values, life style, unique personality, and, thus, his or her unique style of teaching. However, it is possible to identify four basic concepts of teaching which characterize most of the underlying values held by American teachers.[3]

Dispensing Information

On the extreme left of the continuum is the oldest concept of teaching (and still the most common), which holds that the role of the teacher is one of dispensing information. The concept assumes that there is a clearly identifiable and transmittable body of knowledge that constitutes the content of formal education, and that learning consists of acquiring as much of the knowledge as possible. Thus there are definite standards of achievement which determine the degree to which a student is a success or failure. Failure is not mastering the subject matter, and the teacher is the authority over right or wrong. As a result, the teacher is the focal point of the classroom. If extroverted, she or he lectures, amplifies, and explains; if shy, she or he relies more on readings and electronic aids. In either case, the teacher determines what is important and what is correct. The result of this process is dependency on the authority of the teacher for determining "truth."

Changing Behavior

The next teaching style on the expository side is based on theories of social engineering and programmed learning proposed recently by B. F. Skinner and others, and on earlier theories of conditioning by J. B. Watson and A. H. Thorndike. This concept assumes that the role of the teacher is to facilitate or cause the student's behavior to change. Actual teaching consists of establishing specific objectives, and then designing tasks through which the student can accomplish these objectives. Learning is viewed as incremental, sequential, and task oriented. The "behavior changer" usually uses kits, workbooks, duplicated sheets, and/or, if funds are available, sophisticated equipment. The task is to diagnose, prescribe, and monitor the student's progress through a systematic sequence of tasks. The teaching role is basically one of checking the work of individual students, answering questions, providing feedback and reinforcement, evaluating success, and prescribing new programs. Contracts are frequently used to give students a sense of achievement. The "information dispenser" knows what the students *need to know,* and the "behavior changer" knows what it is they *need to be able to do.* Currently, this concept is in vogue, supported by educators who promote "accountability" and "competency-based instruction."

Self-Actualization

At the extreme right of the continuum is the concept of self-actualization. This concept is based on the premise that the task of the teacher is to stimulate each student to achieve full self-realization. The teacher's role is nondirective and the students assume responsibility for their own education. Each student determines what she or he wants to learn and the teacher helps her or him learn it. There is little predetermined structure to the learning process—the teacher and student develop the structure as they go. High priority is given to interpersonal communication and self-direction. Personal responses, honesty, and immediate feedback are highly valued, and individual creativity is considered extremely important. The teacher encourages all forms of student self-expression, art, music, manual skills, drama, improvisation, and creative writing. Teacher-planned structured group activity of any kind is avoided, and spontaneity and student-initiated and directed activity are encouraged. The teacher strives for an atmosphere of mutual support and trust by talking honestly, openly, and freely and listening intently. There are no right or wrong answers, only honest and dishonest ones.

Although currently there are few classrooms where this concept of teaching is clearly evident, there is a growing body of literature, and a concomitant emphasis is being placed on providing an educational atmosphere that facilitates creative thought and open interpersonal relationships. This is an encouraging trend.

Inquiry

In general the concept of inquiry is based on the assumption that the teacher's role is one of structuring the learning environment to encourage students to generate and test their own ideas of meaning. "Process" is as much or more important than "content." Emphasis is not on subject matter to be mastered, but rather on ways of examining and explaining phenomena. There are no teacher-determined "correct" outcomes. The students are encouraged to test the usefulness of their own ideas by applying them to new problem situations.

However, locating inquiry on the teaching continuum requires first describing more precisely the meanings that have been given to this ambiguous word. More often than not inquiry symbolizes different things to different people. The meanings that educators have for the term lie on a continuum also—from highly controlled teacher-guided discussion to completely autonomous student trial-and-error discovery:

TEACHING CONTINUUM

EXPOSITION   DISCOVERY
(CLOSED)   (OPEN)

INQUIRY CONTINUUM

TEACHER-CONTROLLED
DISCUSSION   DISCOVERY

Robert Glaser has found two different patterns in instructional sequences called "discovery." One sequence has the teacher guiding the discussion in such a way that the student induces the generalization and then tests it by applying it; the second is a relatively unguided sequence to which learners apply their own structure. The first is characterized by inductive processes, the second by trial and error.[4]

J. Richard Suchman considers inquiry to be a fundamental and natural process of learning by which an individual gathers information, raises and tests hypotheses, and builds theories and tests them empirically. Suchman considers this to be an intuitive process which is evident in the young child and continues as a basic form of learning throughout life. However, he has found that the conditions that normally occur in the classroom do not facilitate its presence. He points out that while inquiry is controlled by the learner, the conditions by which it occurs must be provided by the teacher: "It is possible for a teacher to engineer conceptual reorganization in a child and to bring about the child's accommodation to discrepant events by programming a series of experiences, by drawing on past experiences and by focusing attention through verbal instruction and exposition on selected aspects of his environment."[5]

The Suchman method is located on the right of the inquiry continuum. It is a process in which the teacher presents a problem in the form of a discrepant event (where there is no immediate and obvious explanation for the phenomenon) and each individual student is encouraged to generate theories (explanations of cause), using the teacher as a source of information to verify or support the theory. The teacher does not have a content or subject matter goal in mind. The teacher's goal is to assist each student to progress as far as she or he is ready and able to go in the process of observing the event, acquiring data about the event, generating ideas of what caused the event to happen, and then testing the usefulness of the ideas. There are no right and wrong answers. All ideas are accepted, regardless of how "scientific" or useful the idea might be considered by the teacher. The whole purpose is to help each child seek and test *her* or *his* answers to the problems.

Fred E. Newton, in his manual on facilitating the Suchman form of inquiry, states: "When students use a rational process to build and test ideas about the world, they are matching a generalization of judgment (theory) they've made against evidence (data) they've collected. They decide on their own match. This is different from giving students generalizations. It is also different from telling students their idea is wrong, or right, for that matter."[6]

Inquiry as a Guided Discussion   On the other, left-hand side of the inquiry continuum is this program. It, too, is based on the belief that the process of inquiry is a natural and normal learning pattern in each individual. In addition, the program assumes that this natural process can be facilitated by the teacher through a process of guided discussion, that the strategies necessary to conduct such a discussion are relatively easily learned, and that they can be facilitated with groups of students as well as with individuals.

The specific teaching strategies for conducting such a discussion, and the application of the process to curriculum content, are presented sequentially and incrementally in the following chapters. However, in summary, the concept of inquiry is one in which the learner:

1. *Confronts a problem.* The problem can be quite individual and personal in nature; however, more generally, it is posed by the teacher, or cooperatively generated by the students, and focuses on the curriculum content of the class.

2. *Acquires information.* A knowledge base of information related to all elements of the problem is generated.

3. *Analyzes relationships.* Comparative and cause-and-effect relationships between elements of the problem are carefully examined.

4. *Generates ideas.* Explanations of cause and effect are stated.

5. *Tests ideas.* The ideas are examined to determine their usefulness in accounting for other, similar situations, or in predicting the future accurately. Also known as tests for validity and reliability.

Basically, inquiry, as presented here, is the scientific process by which knowledge is generated and validated. It is a learning process in which students are confronted with a "problem"—a discrepancy or a puzzle for which a solution is not obviously evident—and, by gathering information and analyzing relationships between and within areas of information, they generate ideas of explanation and subsequently test them to assess their usefulness.

Matters of Self-Concept and Personal Style

A very basic difference between any form of inquiry method and the expository methods of teaching is in relation to the source from which learners derive their feelings of self-worth. All of us need to feel successful and wanted. Hermits may have decided they don't need people, but chances are they chose their life of isolation because they weren't receiving the kind of good feeling one gets from having others approve of one and what one does. Much of the good feelings we have about ourselves comes from rewards given by someone else. It's called *extrinsic motivation*. We get an A, or a smile, or a clap on the back, or some kind of real or symbolic M & M from someone we've pleased. Most of us have gone through a school system based on this sort of motivational process. Other than the danger of placing the learner in a continuously dependent position, it's not really a "bad" thing. In fact, there are many things, like conjugating a verb and memorizing the times tables, for which it's really the only reason we accomplish the task.

On the other hand, there's another reason for learning. It's what Suchman calls the "motivation of curiosity."[7] It's based on the human need to bring about a balance, or equilibrium, in our understanding of what works and why things function as they do. When people see something in their lives that just doesn't quite seem right, they have an innate desire to try to make it right, or at least understand why it isn't. ("Where is that weird smell coming from?" "What makes you believe such a thing?" "Why are you mad at him?" "What makes it keep turning off?") We get our intellectual "kicks" by finally being able to exclaim, "Ah-hah! Now I see why!" It's called *intrinsic motivation*. It's doing the task because it is personally satisfying, personally interesting, and personally rewarding. The problem solver may want to share the solution, but the real pleasure comes from having solved the problem, whether anyone else appreciates it or not. That's basic to inquiry.

Which Is Best?

To attempt empirically to support the value of inquiry in any form as superior to all other styles of teaching is futile. The research in teaching and learning is simply not that good. That is not just the biased impression of this writer, but a view expressed by many. In a recent article, a former U.S. Commissioner of Education, Howard Howe II, among other critical comments on the state of educational research, makes the following point in comparing educational research with research in technological fields:

> If we can go to the moon through the miracles of R & D, then why on earth can't we figure out the most advantageous class size, or the results of increasing expenditures on schools, or the effects of integration, or how to teach children to read? The answer is, of course, that these problems which worry educators and for which they seek definite answers through research are vastly more complex than the relatively simple matter of going to the moon. In education, the fundamental units with which we deal are individual human beings whose behavior is influenced by differing inheritances, by varied experiences in life, and by feelings and attitudes that are unpredictable and changing as life experiences change. Information about human beings cannot be put into computers with the expectation that calculations about them will have the predictability that the laws of gravity will produce when fed into the same computers.[8]

INQUIRY IN PERSPECTIVE

Edwin Fenton, after visiting more than thirty social studies curriculum projects throughout the United States, and after reading countless reports, articles, and books on research studies in educational methodology, reports:

No final answers to basic questions about teaching have yet emerged, perhaps because assessing the effectiveness of teaching poses enormously complicated problems. Three of the many complications may make the issue clear.

In the first place, teachers vary. Two teachers employing the same strategy may produce noticeably different results with their students. Strategies which fail with one teacher flourish with another. A teacher's warmth, his interest in his work, his knowledge of his subject, his feelings about young people, his personality, his facility with words — all these attributes, and many others, have an impact upon teaching.

In the second place, the same strategy will affect children in different ways. The best illustration of this principle comes from students of different ages. In order to grasp the meaning of new concepts, young children need concrete, specific, manipulative examples. . . . But beginning somewhere in the junior high years, students are able to grasp abstractions without direct experience. Hence, verbal learning by expository teaching techniques can be defended for older children while it has little utility for children in the elementary years.

In the third place, the effect of a teaching strategy must be measured by an evaluation instrument. Most tests given in the schools measure acquisition of knowledge, and, on the whole, measure it quite well. But tests to measure the ability of a mode of inquiry . . . are conspicuously absent from most social studies classrooms.[9]

It seems you might select any teaching style and be content that you are teaching in a manner which can be as well supported theoretically and empirically as any other. *Not really!* It's not that easy. Despite the inadequacy of the research, and the relative validity of Fenton's statements, each of us must make choices as to what kind of a person we wish to be, what kind of a teacher we wish to be, and what kind of students we wish to develop. If we consider ourselves to be professional, then those choices had better be based on values that can be supported, philosophically and ethically, if not empirically. Hopefully, part of the decision will be based on what one considers desirable learning behavior. There is some fairly good evidence to support the belief that the "type of teaching" produces, or at least influences significantly, the "type of learning." Marshall B. Rosenberg, of the Seattle, Washington, schools, identified clearly the following styles of learners in that district.[10] (I think all experienced teachers will be able to draw a relationship between each classification and particular children they have in their classroom right now.)

1.   *Rigid-inhibited style.* Problem-solving behavior is characterized by a rigid, dogmatic adherence to absolutistic principles. When absolutistic principles are not available and the child is confronted with ambiguous or complex problem-solving situations, he or she is likely to become confused, disoriented, or withdrawn.

TEACHING CONTINUUM

EXPOSITION ◄──► DISCOVERY

Dispensing Information	*Changing Behavior*	*Inquiry*	*Self-Actualization*
There is a clearly identifiable and transmittable body of information.	Terminal behaviors are specified in advance.	Students generate and test their own meaning. Process is as important as content.	Students determine personal goals. High priority on effective interpersonal communication and self-direction.
Learning consists of remembering as much of the knowledge as possible.	Learning is incremental, sequential, and task oriented.	Learning consists of concept development and generating and testing ideas of cause and effect. No closure of ideas.	Learning consists of attempting to achieve full self-realization.
Teacher's role is to dispense information and serve as judge over what is right or wrong.	Teacher's role is to cause students' behavior to change. Teacher diagnoses, prescribes, monitors, assesses, and provides feedback.	Teacher's role is to pose problems, provide resources, facilitate process, and help test the validity of ideas generated. No teacher-determined right or wrong answers.	Teacher's role is nondirective and facilitative, to create an atmosphere of mutual support and trust. No right or wrong answers, only honest or dishonest ones.

2. *Undisciplined style.* Problem-solving behavior is characterized by weak tolerance for frustration; exploitive, coercive, and manipulative interpersonal relationships; and primary interest in hedonistic gratification. The child seeks personal gratification and attempts to avoid responsibility, causing problems in relating to authority. When confronted with a problem, the child is unable to mobilize energy in a goal-directed way.

3. *Acceptance-anxious style.* Problem-solving behavior is characterized by excessive concern with external evaluation of performance. The child is often so concerned about how others feel about him or her that he or she cannot function. At times the child is a "good Joe," at other times the child is extremely competitive. The child is more comfortable in a passive learning situation where the teacher presents the right answer than in an active learning situation where she or he has to formulate ideas. (I have to admit that I often

CHART 1-2

THEORIES	BEHAVIORISM	HUMANISM
TRUTH	Authority lies outside of self.	Authority lies within self.
LEARNING	Process of acquiring knowledge and skills. Learner is acted on by outside forces, is a product of stimulus and response.	Process of generating and testing personal meaning. The mind possesses an innate order-generating capacity, a built-in drive to learn.
INSTRUC-TIONAL GOALS	Cultural transmission. Developing knowledge and skills. Developing products.	Building positive self-concept. Generating and testing personal meaning. Developing the person.
PROBLEM SOLVING	When confronted with a problem (technological, scientific, or human) is able to recall and use previously learned knowledge and skills.	When confronted with a problem (technological, scientific, or human) is able to generate data, analyze relationships, generate an explanation or solution, and test explanation or solution.
REINFORCE-MENT	Immediate reward for correct behavior. Incorrect behavior is ignored if possible. Punishment is avoided if possible.	Reinforcement is always in the form of feedback reports. Judgments are always accompanied by criteria. Language is nonjudgmental when dealing with student-generated ideas and values. Incorrect and inappropriate behavior is not ignored.
MOTIVATION	Based on extrinsic rewards. Teacher rewards desired behavior with praise, symbols, or privileges. Ignores incorrect behavior or applies mild aversion stimuli.	Based on intrinsic rewards. Students are involved in goal setting and self-assessment. Teacher behavior is facilitative, accepting, supporting, and trusting.
HUMAN RELA-TIONSHIPS	Gamesmanship.	Accepting, trusting, and risk taking.
PROPONENTS	Watson, Thorndike, Skinner.	Maslow, Rogers, Combs, Glaser.

function at this level. I'd like to think that I'm becoming a fully functioning, self-actualizing person, but I'm not there yet.)

4.   *Creative style.* Problem-solving behavior is characterized by the ability to be goal directed as well as reflective and self-critical at the same time. The child is open to new experiences, and is not afraid to try something new or to consider several alternatives. The child is able to carefully evaluate herself or himself, and with little anxiety accept and profit from mistakes.

The Challenge of Choice

It should not be inferred that there is a "proven" relationship between the styles of teaching and these styles of learning. Nevertheless, there obviously is a relationship between the way teachers teach and the way students learn. Consequently, the question that begs to be asked is: "How can teachers provide the conditions that will facilitate more of the creative, problem-solving style of learning?" It is ridiculous to propose that the inquiry method will *always* produce creative learners, and that it should be used as the predominant form of teaching regardless of content and level. Obviously, information dispensing is a useful, sensible way to teach when one needs to dispense information. Behavior changing is obviously the most logical and effective method when one is interested in changing behavior. However, I believe that the inquiry approach to learning is not nearly as evident in classrooms as it should be. One of the many challenges that we teachers face is to pick the right method, or combination of methods, to accomplish our desired instructional goal. Hopefully, this book will provide the understandings and skills that you need in order to make greater use of the inquiry method in your classroom.

Source Notes

1. Herbert A. Thelen, *Education and the Human Quest* (Chicago: University of Chicago Press, 1972), pp. 22–23.

2. Edwin Fenton, *The New Social Studies* (New York: Holt, Rinehart and Winston, 1967), p. 33.

3. With the exception of inquiry, the descriptions of concepts are summarized from Ronald LaConte, "Styles of Teaching," *Professional Report* (May 1974).

4. Robert Glaser, "Variables in Discovery Learning," in *Learning by Discovery, A Critical Appraisal*, eds. Lee S. Schulman and Evan R. Keoslar (Chicago: Rand-McNally, 1966), pp. 13–26.

5. J. Richard Suchman, "A Child and the Inquiry Process" (paper presented at the Eighth ASCD Curriculum Research Institute, Western Section, Anaheim, Calif., December 3, 1962).

6. Fred E. Newton, *Facilitating Inquiry in the Classroom* (Portland, Oreg.: Northwest Regional Educational Laboratory, 1970), p. 51.

7. J. Richard Suchman, *Developing Inquiry* (Chicago: Science Research Associates, 1975), p. 71.

8. Harold Howe II, "What's Wrong with Research in Education?" *Today's Education* (September–October 1976), p. 29.

9. Fenton, op. cit., pp. 32–33.

10. Marshall B. Rosenberg, *Diagnostic Teaching* (Seattle: Special Child Publications, 1968).

2

Tuning In on Language

Overview

Rationale

To successfully implement the instructional process of inquiry, the teacher must be particularly sensitive to the meanings that students have for the words they use. The goal for an inquiry lesson is determined in advance by the teacher, but the strategy for achieving that goal is based largely on cues received from the verbal responses of the students. Teachers must recognize that the words *they* use, and the words *students* use, have meanings that are unique to the individual speaking. If effective communication is to occur, techniques must be employed to ensure a *minimum* of misunderstanding and confusion and a *maximum* of "tuning in" to the personal meanings of an individual's words.

General Objectives

At the conclusion of this chapter, you should be able to identify highly inferential and judgmental words and to employ specific techniques to determine the unique meanings each person has for the words she or he uses. More specifically, this chapter is designed to create the conditions by which you develop:

- Sensitivity to the confusing nature of word meanings, and an understanding of the need to check on the personal meanings that students have for the words they use.

- Ability to discriminate between language statements composed of words with commonly agreed-on meanings and statements composed of words with un-validated inferential or judgmental meanings.

- Ability to check on personal meaning by effectively employing the techniques of asking for personal meaning, paraphrasing, and asking for illustrations.

Language Sensitivity: The Foundation of Effective Teaching

Can Humans Survive?

Of all the animals on earth, only humans have developed the means for rational problem solving and decision making. Only humans have developed ways of coding and decoding sounds into symbolic systems of communication — language — that allow the storage, sharing, and use of information. Symbols make it possible to describe the past, explain the present, and predict the future. Symbolic thought and behavior give meaning to human existence.[1]

But you may reasonably ask, "Why, then, are humans apparently not able to utilize this ability to communicate to deal constructively with the issues created by their very existence?" It is relatively easy to identify and list the major problems that American society faces in the present decade. The number-one health problem is mental illness — more Americans suffer from mental illness than from all other forms of illness combined. Another serious problem is that of crime. Another is suicide. A less publicized but startlingly widespread problem is that of damaged children — the most common cause of infant mortality in the United States is parental beating. Still another problem involves access to reliable information — the "credibility gap" in crucial areas of society and government. There are the problems of civil rights, electronic bugging, sex, drugs, population growth, abortions, housing, food and water supply, pollution, urban life, foreign aid, and a mountain of problems stemming from the alleged Communist conspiracy.[2]

A fundamental problem underlying all these social issues is in the symbolic process itself. That is, in order to understand and deal with the world effectively, we must comprehend and be skillful in dealing with the semantic dimension of language.

A World of Symbols

A prerequisite to any clear comprehension of semantic functions is the recognition that we deal with both a *real world* and a *verbal world*. Our real world is that which we experience directly. Our verbal world is made up of the words we use and those that come to us as reports or reports of reports (history) of the real world. The verbal world, then, is the creation of the symbolic process, the process that allows humans to arbitrarily make infinite combinations of certain sounds or marks stand for a universe of other things. However, some basic problems of communication arise from the fact that there is no necessary connection between the symbol and that which is symbolized. The problems would not exist if learning language were simply a matter of learning words that God or nature had somehow *attached* to each of the possible referents in the real world. But language has "meaning" only by virtue of a tenuous, imperfect, and shifting set of agreements among humans that a given symbol will *arbitrarily* stand for a given referent.

Symbol Uniqueness

The learning of language is an abstracting or conceptualizing process to acquire a set of language symbols whose meanings are in some measure unique to the individual expressing the symbol. Consider a small toddler standing on a street corner with his father. The child points to something moving down the street and his father says, "Car, Billy. Car." The child says "car" and receives a smile and pat on the head, which he deserves. Something else moves down the street and the child responds with "car" but receives the comment, "No, son, that's a truck."

Thus Billy is beginning a set of discriminating experiences in the process of using language to represent the real world. The language learning process moves through sequential and developmental phases as the individual adds new sensory and verbal information from the external world and incorporates it into his or her internal and/or verbal world. At the same time his or her words become increasingly abstract and inclusive as more events or elements are added and accommodated to the total. However, at any point in a person's development, when he or she utters the symbol "car" or "vehicle" or "transportation," the *meaning* of that symbol— exactly what it stands for in the person's internal world—is known only to that individual. The usefulness of the word (or any word), for communicating, depends on the extent to which what it symbolizes for Billy approximates what it symbolizes for the person with whom he is communicating. But, just as important, the word's usefulness in organizing and guiding Billy's responses to the world depends on the extent to which its meaning inside Billy's head accurately matches the referent in the real world.

To illustrate these two important points, let's assume that Billy has grown into adolescence. We overhear him saying to his father, "Pop, I need you to lay the wheels on me tonight so I can make it with this stone fox from Washington." Translated into standard English, Billy's statement means, "I hope you will let me use the family car tonight so I can keep my date with an especially good-looking girl from Washington High School." But since Billy hasn't used standard English, the chances are that his communication to his father will fail because Billy's meanings for the words he uses are too different from his father's meanings for the same words.

Let's pursue our imaginary case a bit further to illustrate the second point. Billy, in his anxiety to have a successful date, to make a good impression on his "stone fox," invests half a dollar in a small booklet entitled *How to Be a Lady's Man,* and has read it cover to cover. He is not sure he entirely understands the book, but its tone is authoritative, so he resolves to follow its advice. Later, Billy comes home early from his date with one very swollen eye—the result of behaving toward a real girl as if she were the hypothetical, verbally created symbol that got into Billy's head from the booklet. When our verbal world fails significantly to match the real world, we are likely to be in trouble. Or, to put it another way, maladjustment and malfunctioning occur when words do not accurately symbolize the real world or when words symbolize different things to different people. To assume that the symbols in our verbal world are exact counterparts of items of experience in the real world is to court disaster. By the same token, to say dogmatically that we know what a word means when we hear it spoken by another is nonsense. We know what it means to us, and we may know *approximately* what it means to another, depending on the extent to which the word has commonly agreed-on referents in the real world, but we never know *exactly* the personal meaning given to the symbol by the speaker. We can only *interpret* what has been said in light of both verbal and physical contexts, and act according to our intepretation.

Nonlogical Logic

Another, rather monumental problem in decoding language symbols lies in the Aristotelian logic that characterizes Western rational thought patterns. This form of logic considers the symbol as fixed and immutable, thus meaning the same to all individuals. For example, *honesty* means never taking anything that does not belong to you (and therefore does not characterize the Eskimo cultural pattern of helping yourself when in need to your neighbor's wood and meat supply). A *functional* house in Western culture is one that will withstand all reasonably predictable natural conditions. A Japanese house, on the other hand, is *functional* in relation to daily livability rather than to a capacity to endure against natural violence such as typhoons and earthquakes. Every year, in Japan, howling winds send many roofs flying, and a large number of people lose their homes in torrential floods, but the Japanese attitude is one of harmonizing rather than opposing natural forces. We have a tendency to say the Japanese are "crazy" not to construct homes that would withstand nearly any natural force. However, the beliefs that people are a natural part of their environment and that the environment has spiritual as well as material composition result in the value of living as a *part* of nature rather than *apart* from nature. *Functional,* therefore, in at least this one context, has profoundly different meanings in Japanese and Western cultures.

There are many subcultures in our own Western society that attach their own "rational" and "logical" meanings to particular words. Consider the controversy in America around such symbols as *love, responsibility, loyalty, justice,* and *patriotism,* to name just a few.

Part of the difficulty undoubtedly stems from the fact that many individuals react to the symbol as though it were the object or event itself. For a broader example, let's consider the term *murderer,* which automatically results in social censure for the individual thus labeled. By cultural definition, a murderer is an individual tried and convicted of taking the life of an ingroup member. However, socially approved killing has occurred throughout human history, and continues to occur every day. It is socially approved because its victims are members of an outgroup. Often, such killing is labeled *heroism.* Yet the act is the same. A human life has been taken. But the word used to describe the act results in either social censure or social approval. We react to the *word,* and not the act. We may be startled into awareness of this tendency only when something like the My Lai Massacre trials force us to consider the fragile and largely semantic distinction between heroism and murder. "People need to be scientifically aware of the powers and limitations of symbols, especially words, if they are to guard against being driven into complete bewilderment by the complexity of the semantic environment."[3]

Masquerading Statements: Feelings and Commands

Another problem of communication involves the need to discriminate between words that communicate information and words that communicate feelings.

Much of the verbal interaction between individuals has a basic affective or feeling character. Quite often the feeling is expressed in a manner that makes it easily recognized as feeling:

TUNING IN ON LANGUAGE

"I'm crazy about that beautiful home."

"I really respect Mr. Jones."

"Man, I feel sick about that test."

However, one of the very tricky things about language is that one kind of language statement often masquerades as another. Look, for example, at these two statements:

"A lizard is a reptile."

"Johnny is a rotten kid."

The forms of the statements are identical. Both are stated in a form we commonly use for conveying information, *describing.* In this example, the first sentence does just that. But the second is masquerading. It seems to be communicating information but, of course, its real function is to express a feeling—which in this case is also a judgment. (It is worthwhile to take a good look at the verb in the example sentences. General semanticists call it "the *is* of identity" and they encourage us to avoid it in our language behavior because it leads itself so easily to the kind of masquerading exemplified above.)

A second common type of masquerading statement is the command, or *direction,* which pretends to be something else. Suppose that the teacher says, "Harold, I was wondering if you would like to open the window for us." Ostensibly the teacher has just offered a description of his own thought process, that is, in form, the sentence seems designed merely to convey information—"This is what I was just wondering," and Harold might technically be justified to sit still and reply, "Oh, were you?" But, fortunately, Harold sees through the masquerade or, rather, he has learned to recognize this pattern as one of the common ways in which teachers give commands.

Let's examine the following statement of a teacher in a third-grade classroom.

"Boys and girls, I hear talking. I'd hate to have people in here this noon writing out their. times tables."

If we analyze this language statement we find again that it appears to exemplify the process we have called *describing.*

"Boys and girls, I hear talking." (This simply gives information or describes what is heard.)

"I'd hate to have people in here this noon writing out their times tables." (This describes a value preference or choice: the teacher chooses not to have kids in during the noon hour. Whether valued for the kids' sake or the teacher's sake is not clear.)

The message conveyed in this total statement can easily be interpreted as *directing.* It is apparent that the teacher is attempting to control the students or to influence them to get busy, threatening them with confinement and the times tables in order to obtain this behavior.

If we had to rely solely on this teacher's statement to determine the meaning, we might conclude that it is really just describing a casual preference. But we (and the students) have enough clues of content to be pretty certain that the statement is intended to be directive.

The point is, when interpreting feelings or intentions that occur in a great many language statements, the only effective way to assess intended meanings is to apply more than just listening.

The Language of the Classroom

You do not need to spend a great deal of time in a school classroom to find that the patterns of miscommunication that exist in society generally are dramatically evident in the interaction between teachers and students. With the possible exception of an occasional involvement in a science laboratory experiment and the rare experience of a field trip, students spend their entire time in school dealing with a highly abstract verbal world. To a large extent they are expected to consider *the* definition or meaning of a word rather than the *meanings* of a word. They are expected to accept the interpretation of the teacher or the textbook as though it were actually the real world event itself. In short, students are expected to deal with abstractions that only to a very limited degree symbolize the world that exists now or the world that existed in the past. The "insanity" of the classroom occurs when the teacher gives the impression to students that the real world is being considered rather than interpretations.

The following verbatim quote is an example of a common classroom statement. This statement concluded a discussion of the American U-2 spy plane that was shot down over Russia.

Well now, this is one thing that we will, perhaps, have to judge all of these different facts now that have been revealed. Certainly, the first set of facts show the United States officials said one thing and the day after that they reversed themselves, so we'll just have to take the facts as they develop and try to determine that which is right. I think now that on Sunday we'll have a full summary article, because the Sunday paper is usually very good for this.

The teacher's intent was probably to encourage the students to explore different opinions and predict possible results. However, the language used suggests that adequate "facts" are available to them (which they almost never are), that the Sunday paper is a source of such facts, and that final conclusions or complete explanations can be formulated (which is impossible — predictions perhaps — but not complete explanations).

How much better it would have been if the teacher had recognized the tentative and personal nature of interpretations and judgments, and, instead of the above, had said:

We have considered some conflicting reports about the incident as interpreted by newspaper writers and television commentators. Officials, according to these reporters, appear to have reversed themselves. We need to look for additional in-

formation before forming our own personal judgments. The Sunday paper may be a good place to look for other interpretations of this event.

It is small wonder that many—perhaps most—students eventually feel that school is a place where you deal with things that either do not really exist or are irrelevant, a place where you are required to "put in your time" until the bell rings and the real world becomes excitingly and meaningfully available.

Tuning In on Language

The inquiry process involves the teacher's becoming a facilitator to aid students to generate and test their own interpretations of the world. It is not a process whereby the teacher *tells* the students what is right or wrong—the *truth*—it is a process in which the teacher helps the students discover meaning for themselves. To do so, it is essential that the teacher develop sensitivity to, understanding of, and skill in dealing with the semantic structure of language. The following activities are designed to develop that sensitivity, understanding, and skill in the processes of "tuning in on language."

Report Words vs. Inferential-Judgmental Words

A way to improve communication is to examine language in relation to what S. I. Hayakawa has termed *report words, inferential words,* and *judgmental words:*[4]

1. *Reports.* These are statements that describe what a person has seen, heard, or felt. They are accurate descriptions of a personal observation or measurement. They are verifiable. At the highest level they are the language of science; at the lowest level they are descriptions using words with commonly agreed-on referents in the real world. They exclude, as far as possible, inferences and judgments. For example:

    "The car is light blue, with chrome wheels and trim."

    Not: **"The car is beautifully finished and trimmed."**

    "His face turned red after you made that statement."

    Not: **"You made him very angry."**

2. *Inferences.* These are statements about the unknown made on the basis of the known. The following statements could have been made by individuals who possessed a good deal of descriptive information as a basis for the statement. However, in each case the statement *infers* a situation that may or may not be so.

    "He's afraid of girls."

    "She has an inferiority complex."

"Russia intends to control the world."

"You made him very angry."

Also, in each case the statement includes highly ambiguous terms that have unique personal meaning for the person speaking. *Inferences* only have meaning to the listener when they are presented as inferences and are followed by *report statements* that clarify the personal meaning of the terms being used. For example:

"It seems to me that he's afraid of girls. (He never talks to them, he never asks a girl out, and he avoids going to places where girls are likely to be present.)"

3. *Judgments.* These are statements that express approval or disapproval of occurrences, persons, or objects.

"That's a lousy book."

"What a beautiful house."

"The Toyota Corolla is a great car."

"He's a thief." (Both an inference and a judgment.)*

Each statement leaves the listener uncertain as to what the speaker has observed, felt, or heard that leads to the belief expressed. The judgment only becomes meaningful to the listener when the statement also describes the basis for the judgment in report language. For example:

"The Toyota Corolla is a great car. It has both fast acceleration and low gas consumption."

Thus, when speaking or writing, the use of report language enhances mutual understanding. Without clarifying report statements, the use of *inferential-judgmental* language often inhibits understanding.

EXERCISES: TUNING IN ON WORDS

The following exercises are designed to provide practice in discriminating between words and statements that can be classified either as: (1) reports, or (2) inferences and/or judgments. The key is: (1) *Report statement*—does the statement *describe* an occurrence, object, or person using words with commonly agreed-on meanings? (2) *Inferential-judgmental statement*—does the statement make unvalidated inferences and/or judgments using words with highly personal meanings?

* It is not uncommon for a judgmental statement to be given in the form of both an inference and a judgment. In this case the statement *infers* that he is a thief and also implies a negative value or judgment about thievery.

TUNING IN ON LANGUAGE

Directions

Read the following statements and classify each by coding in the blank space either:

R—Report statement, or

I-J—Inferential-judgmental statement

_____ 1. The temperature outside is 89 degrees Fahrenheit.

_____ 2. He's a typical politician.

_____ 3. The new styles are really neat.

_____ 4. Japanese are very polite.

_____ 5. The car didn't stop when the light turned red.

_____ 6. Subtraction is really tough!

_____ 7. He's driving recklessly.

_____ 8. Kids accept more responsibility if they are treated as human beings.

_____ 9. She left the meeting before it was over.

_____10. I asked him three times to take out the garbage and it's still under the sink.

Answers and Explanations

____R____ 1. This statement is made with words that can be classified as *scientific report language.*

____I-J____ 2. "Typical politician" is probably both an *inference* and a *judgment.* The speaker has made an inference from the subject's behavior and has then applied a label that carries, for most of us, an implied (negative) judgment. We are not told what behavior was observed.

____I-J____ 3. An obvious *judgment.* It merely expresses approval without clarifying what is approved of, or why.

____I-J____ 4. Many individuals (including this writer) have a tendency to classify this as a report statement on the basis of personal experience. However, it is a *judgment,* attributing to the subject a characteristic valued positively, without describing the behavior on which the attribution is based.

____R____ 5. A fairly obvious *report* statement. A description of an event using words with commonly agreed-upon meanings.

____I-J____ 6. A *judgment,* based on an individual's experience, which may differ radically from that of another individual. Also, the word "tough" is a highly ambiguous term that needs report language to clarify its meaning.

<u>I-J</u> 7. An *inference* and *judgment*. "Recklessly" is a highly inferential judgmental term.

<u>I-J</u> 8. An *inference* without report statements to support its validity.

<u>R</u> 9. A clear descriptive statement of what was observed.

<u>R</u> 10. A report statement. (Not uncommonly heard in this writer's household.)

Directions

Again, try to discriminate between report statements and inferential-judgmental statements. Classify each by coding in the blank space either:

R—Report statement, or

I-J—Inferential-judgmental statement

_____ 1. Jimmy can't be trusted.

_____ 2. She was sitting and looking out the window, not hearing a thing.

_____ 3. He looked at his neighbor's paper twice during the test.

_____ 4. The problem with Jane is that her voice turns people off.

_____ 5. Bill's house is three blocks from the corner, is two stories tall, and has green shutters on the windows.

_____ 6. It's really a neat house.

_____ 7. There's no question in my mind, he's a Communist.

_____ 8. The car accelerated 1,000 feet in 3 seconds.

_____ 9. Kids today just will not assume responsibility.

_____ 10. She was bored by the meeting.

Answers and Explanations

<u>I-J</u> 1. "Jimmy can't be trusted" is both an *inference* and a *judgment*. There is nothing in the statement that validates the assertion by describing the behavior on which it is based.

<u>I-J</u> 2. The first part of this statement can be classified as a report, but the last phrase, "not hearing a thing," makes it an *inference.*

<u>R</u> 3. A definite *report* statement. The speaker is describing an observation.

<u>I-J</u> 4. An unvalidated *inference.* There is nothing that describes the basis for the statement.

<u>R</u> 5. A clear *report* in unambiguous, commonly used, and understood language.

_____I-J___ 6. This statement is an obvious *judgment* without supporting report statements.

_____I-J___ 7. An *inference* and a *judgment*. Name-calling is almost invariably judgmental, and usually inferential as well.

_____R___ 8. Assuming that scientific instruments were used to measure the acceleration, this is an obvious *report* statement.

_____I-J___ 9. A not uncommonly heard *inference* and *judgment*.

_____I-J___10. An unsupported *inference*.

ACTIVITIES: TUNING IN ON WORDS

The following activities are designed to make you more sensitive to the words people use when speaking and writing.

1. Listen carefully to conversations between people (at dinner, over coffee, on the bus, etc.). Tune in carefully to the words being used. Attempt to identify the inferential-judgmental statements used and note their effect on the other person. Select one instance and write a short report of it to share with the other class members. Include in your report:

   a. Who was present.

   b. The topic of conversation.

   c. Inferential-judgmental statements noted.

   d. Effect on others.

2. Select an editorial or a letter to the editor from a current newspaper. Read carefully and underline all inferential-judgmental words and statements. Write a brief statement about how you think the author was using these terms in an attempt to influence the reader. Be prepared to share your statement with other members of the class.

Checking for Personal Meaning

It is important to realize that people cannot give, assign, or ascribe meanings that they do not already have in their experience. There is no such thing as a universally accepted meaning of a word. Each word has meaning only insofar as the individual expressing the word gives meaning to it, and she or he can only give meanings that are already in her or his experience. Thus, to talk about what *words* mean, rather than what *people* mean, obscures rather than clarifies the relationship between language and reality. The teacher must recognize that *meaning is not "in words." Meaning is in people, and whatever meanings words have are assigned to them by people.*

Implication for the Classroom   Once the teacher recognizes that there is no inherent meaning in words themselves, that meaning lies within the individual expressing the words, the following implications for the classroom become evident.

1. The need to avoid ever giving children the impression that a word has a single meaning.

    Avoid: "*The* **definition for that word is** _____."

    Avoid: "**What is** *the* **definition of** _____?"

    Ask: "**What do you mean by the word** _____?"

    Ask: "**What different meanings are there for the word** _____?"

    Ask: "**What different meanings does the dictionary give for the word** _____?"

    Ask: "**What comes to mind when you hear the word** _____?"

    Ask: "**Does someone else have a different meaning for the word** _____?"

2. The need to give opportunities for students to build their own word definitions or meanings.

    Ask: "**What does the word** _____ **mean to you?**"

    Ask: "**What meanings can you give for the word** _____?"

3. The need to provide the opportunities for students to compare their meanings of a word with the meanings that others have for the same word.

    Ask: "**Write the meaning to you of the word** _____ **on a piece of paper and we'll share with each other.**"

    Ask: "**What comes to mind when you hear the word** _____?"

4. The need to check on the personal meaning of words being used.

    Ask: "**What do** *you* **mean by the word** _____?" (Asks for personal meaning.)

    Ask: "**By** *revolutionary,* **do you mean someone who throws bombs, or someone who disagrees with the president, or perhaps something else?**" (Paraphrases.)

    Ask: "**Can you give an example of a revolutionary act?**" (Asks for an illustration.)

The following exercises and activities are designed to develop the skills necessary to check on the personal meaning of words being used. Specifically, the skills include: (1) asking for personal meaning, (2) paraphrasing, and (3) asking for illustrations.

Asking for Personal Meaning

One technique for checking on the meaning of a particular word or phrase an individual has used is simply asking, "What do *you* mean by the word(s) _____?" But asking for personal meaning may not be the most effective technique to employ, since the response may come back at the same level of abstraction. For example: "What do you mean, he has communistic tendencies?" Response: "He has a tendency to believe in Communism." However, it is a natural and easy technique to employ with the *usual* results of (1) obtaining an expression that is closer to the referent, that is, that contains more report words and less inferential and judgmental words, and (2) causing the individual to be aware that the listener is interested in what is being said and wants to be certain that she or he understands the communication.

Bear in mind, when asking for personal meaning, that there are two important factors to consider:

1. The question should be asked in a form that implies that there is more than one meaning possible for the term being used. For example:

   Ask: **"What is *your* meaning of the expression 'communistic tendencies'?"**

   Avoid: **"What is *the* meaning of the expression 'communistic tendencies'?"**

2. The response received must be checked to determine if it does actually express in report language what the individual means by the word(s). If the response comes back at the same, or a higher, level of abstraction, probably a different technique needs to be employed to obtain understanding. For example:

   Ask: **"What is your meaning of the expression 'communistic tendencies'?"**

   Response: **"He has a tendency to believe in communism."**

   Since this response is at the same level of abstraction:

   Ask: **"Do you mean, he believes in federal control of the press, or schools, or industry, or did you have something else in mind?"** (Paraphrasing.)

EXERCISES: ASKING FOR PERSONAL MEANING

The following exercises are designed to provide experience in identifying the behavior "asking for personal meaning." Each example has three or more statements that might have been made to check on meaning. However, only one statement accurately asks for the individual's personal meaning. The key is: Does a statement ask for the individual's meaning, implying that there may be several meanings?

Directions

In this exercise, *paraphrasing* and *asking for illustrations* will be evident in the responses given. However, they do not exemplify the desired behavior for this exercise. The correct response in each example will be *"asking for personal meaning."*

Identify which of the statements in each example below accurately illustrates the behavior *asks for personal meaning.* If the statement illustrates the behavior, check *yes.* If not, check *no.*

1. Pupil: "Japan's economy is based on the level of technology."

    a. Teacher: "What is the meaning of level of technology?"

                                                        Yes_____ No_____

    b. Teacher: "By level of technology, do you mean modern machines and farming techniques?"

                                                        Yes_____ No_____

    c. Teacher: "What do you mean by level of technology?"

                                                        Yes_____ No_____

    d. Teacher: "Can you give us an example of what you mean by level of technology?"

                                                        Yes_____ No_____

2. Pupil: "Police officers are good people."

    a. Teacher: "Do you mean they help people cross the street?"

                                                        Yes_____ No_____

    b. Teacher: "What do you mean by good?"

                                                        Yes_____ No_____

    c. Teacher: "Can you tell us what they do that is good?"

                                                        Yes_____ No_____

3. Pupil: "They are inferior people."

    a. Teacher: "What do you mean by inferior?"

                                                        Yes_____ No_____

    b. Teacher: "What is the definition of inferior?"

                                                        Yes_____ No_____

    c. Teacher: "By inferior, do you mean less education, or less intelligence, or something else?"

                                                        Yes_____ No_____

d.   Teacher: "Can you give us an illustration of what you consider to be inferior?"

Yes_____ No_____

Answers and Explanations

1. a.   ___No.___   The teacher asks, "What is *the* meaning of level of technology?" which implies there is only *one* meaning. Remember, there is no such thing as a single meaning of a word, and this impression should never be given to children.

    b.   ___No.___   Here the teacher is paraphrasing—giving two examples and asking if either is correct. It is a good way of checking on meaning but is not the behavior of *asking for personal meaning*.

    c.   ___Yes.___   The question, "What do you mean by level of technology?" clearly asks for personal meaning, implying that there may be other meanings.

    d.   ___No.___   This question is asking for an example or illustration. Again, it is a good way of checking on meaning but is not the behavior of *asking for personal meaning*.

2. a.   ___No.___   Here the teacher is paraphrasing. It is not only not a very good paraphrase, as you will subsequently discover, but also definitely not *asking for personal meaning*.

    b.   ___Yes.___   The question clearly asks for the personal meaning of the word *good.*

    c.   ___No.___   This question asks the child to give a specific illustration. It is an effective technique but not the behavior of *asking for personal meaning*.

3. a.   ___Yes.___   The teacher is clearly asking for the personal meaning of the word *inferior,* implying that there are other meanings.

    b.   ___No.___   This implies that there is only *one* definition—which is not true.

    c.   ___No.___   The teacher is paraphrasing for a check on meaning. In this case it's a good paraphrase. You might wish to check the difference between this statement and that in 2a.

    d.   ___No.___   Here the teacher is clearly asking for a specific illustration.

Directions

Again, identify which of the statements in each example below accurately illustrate the behavior *asks for personal meaning.* If the statement illustrates the behavior, check *yes.* If not, check *no.*

1. Pupil: "These directions are confusing."

a. Teacher: "What do you mean by confusing, Jimmy?"

Yes_____ No_____

b. Teacher: "What is it that's confusing you, Jimmy?"

Yes_____ No_____

c. Teacher: "By confusing, do you mean they are too complicated, or that they have words you don't know, or something else?"

Yes_____ No_____

2. Pupil: "The trouble with Mr. W_____ is that he's just not a competent person."

a. Teacher: "Can you give me an example of what he does that is not competent?"

Yes_____ No_____

b. Teacher: "What's the definition of competent?"

Yes_____ No_____

c. Teacher: "By not competent, do you mean he's not capable?"

Yes_____ No_____

d. Teacher: "What do you mean by competent?"

Yes_____ No_____

3. Pupil: "Driving a car is hazardous to your health."

a. Teacher: "Why do you say that?"

Yes_____ No_____

b. Teacher: "What does hazardous mean to you?"

Yes_____ No_____

c. Teacher: "By hazardous do you mean you could get killed?"

Yes_____ No_____

d. Teacher: "Don't you have your words mixed up?"

Yes_____ No_____

Answers and Explanations

1. a. ___Yes.___ The teacher is clearly asking the pupil to give a personal meaning for the term *confusing.*

b. ___No.___ In this case the student is being asked to give an illustration of what is confusing him or her.

c. ___No.___ This is a paraphrase.

2. a. ___No.___ The pupil is being asked to give an illustration of incompetence.

   b. ___No.___ This implies that there is *one* definition or meaning of competent.

   c. ___No.___ This is a paraphrase, and a very poor one as a matter of fact.

   d. ___Yes.___ This asks for the pupil's personal meaning of competent.

3. a. ___No.___ This is perhaps a natural response, but definitely not a check for meaning.

   b. ___Yes.___ This meets the criteria of asking for personal meaning, with the implication that there can be more than one meaning.

   c. ___No.___ This is a paraphrase.

   d. ___No.___ This is an accusation—and not a check on meaning.

ACTIVITIES: ASKING FOR PERSONAL MEANING

1. Write two examples of a teacher asking a student for the personal meaning of words or phrases just spoken. Be prepared to share with other class members.

2. Engage a personal friend in conversation for the express purpose of practicing the technique of *asking for personal meaning.* (If possible, tape-record the discussion.*) Following the discussion, recall the conversation (or listen to the tape) and identify those instances in which you purposely asked for personal meaning. Then write an example from your conversation that you feel is an accurate illustration of the technique of asking for personal meaning. Be prepared to share your example with other class members.

Paraphrasing

If you tell someone your phone number, the person will usually repeat it to be sure she or he heard it correctly. However, if you make a complicated statement, most people will express agreement or disagreement without trying to be sure they are

---

* Tape-recording a discussion between yourself and another person is not always easy. If it can be done naturally and openly, without any embarrassment, by all means record the conversation since you'll find it very helpful. However, if your friend objects, or if it's embarrassing for you, forget it. Carry on the conversation and try to recall as accurately as possible what was said.

responding to what you intended. Most people seem to assume that what they understand from a statement is what the other intended.

How do you check to be sure that you understand another person's ideas, information, or suggestions as he or she intended them? How do you know that his or her remark means the same to you as it does to him or her?

One way you can get the other person to clarify the remark, as previously indicated, is by simply asking, "What do you mean?" However, as we also saw, it is not uncommon for the response to be given at the same level of abstraction. A more effective technique for checking on meaning is *paraphrasing*.

The Skill   If you state in your own way what the remark conveys to you, the other person can determine whether the message is coming through as intended. Then, if she or he thinks you misunderstand, she or he can speak directly to the specific misunderstanding you have revealed. *Paraphrasing* is a technique *for showing the other person what her or his statement means to you*. It is a way of revealing your understanding of the other person's utterance in order to test your understanding

An additional benefit of paraphrasing is that it lets the other person know that you are interested. It is evidence that you do want to understand what he or she means. If you can convince the other person that you really do understand *his* or *her* point, he or she will probably be more willing to attempt to understand your views.

Paraphrasing, then, helps in two ways to bridge the interpersonal gap: (1) it increases the accuracy of communication, and thus the degree of mutual or shared understanding, and (2) the act of paraphrasing itself conveys feeling—your interest in the other person and your concern to see how the other person views things.

Learning to Paraphrase   People sometimes think of paraphrasing as merely repeating the other person's statement in different terms. Such word swapping may merely result in the illusion of mutual understanding as in the following example:

Sarah: **"Jim should never have become a teacher."**

Fred: **"You mean teaching isn't the right job for him?"**

Sarah: **"Exactly! Teaching is not the right job for Jim."**

Instead of trying to reword Sarah's statement, Fred might have asked himself, "What does Sarah's statement mean to me? What is an *example* of the actual behavior that illustrates the meaning of her statement?" In that case the interchange might have sounded like this:

Sarah: **"Jim should never have become a teacher."**

Fred: **"You mean he is too harsh on the children? Maybe even cruel?"**

Sarah: **"Oh, no. I meant that he has such expensive tastes that he can't ever earn enough as a teacher."**

TUNING IN ON LANGUAGE

Fred: **"Oh, I see. You think he should have gone into a field that would have given him a higher standard of living."**

Sarah: **"Exactly! Teaching is not the right job for Jim."**

Effective paraphrasing is not a trick or a verbal gimmick. It comes from the desire to know what the other means. To satisfy this desire, you reveal the meaning the comment has for you so that the other person can check whether it matches the meaning she or he intended to convey.

When paraphrasing statements of children, two factors must be considered:

1. *The paraphrase should be stated in report language.* The paraphrase should be made with words that have commonly agreed-on meanings. Word swapping, using words at the same level of abstraction, and/or using judgmental or inferential words are inappropriate in any paraphrase—but particularly for children, who are not always secure enough to challenge the teacher's authority. For example:

    Pupil: **"This is a bad book."**

    Teacher: **"By bad, do you mean it's inferior?"**

    Obviously, the student cannot ask back, "By inferior, do you mean bad?" On the other hand, if the paraphrase gives examples using words with commonly agreed-on meanings, the child is in a much stronger position to "disagree," that is, to reject a paraphrase that does not match the intended meaning. For example:

    Pupil: **"This is a bad book."**

    Teacher: **"By bad, do you mean you don't like the story, or the people in the story?"**

    In this case, the student is much more likely to say what she really meant:

    Pupil: **"No, I mean it keeps falling apart."**

2. *The paraphrase should, when possible, present two or more examples.* Many children, as a result of the traditional "teacher-pupil" relationship, have been conditioned to try to *satisfy* the teacher. Some children, even when the paraphrase is given in report language, will *invariably* agree that the teacher's paraphrase is the meaning intended. Giving two or more examples in the paraphrase forces a choice between alternatives, and eventually helps the child gain the security to be able to "correct" the teacher's misperception. For example:

    Pupil: **"We don't get any privileges in this school."**

    Teacher: **"Do you mean because you aren't allowed to run in the halls and run down stairs, or do you have something else in mind?"**

Pupil: **"No, that's okay. I mean we can't ever chew gum or eat candy."**

The act of paraphrasing involves *testing* to see if the meaning that one receives is that which was intended by the speaker. The skill consists of: (1) giving two or more specific examples using words with commonly agreed-on meanings, which illustrates the possible meaning of the speaker's statement, and (2) asking if that meaning is what was intended.

EXERCISES: LEARNING TO PARAPHRASE

Directions

In each of the examples, identify the behavior *paraphrasing*. If the example contains the behavior, check *yes*. If not, check *no*.

1. Pupil: "We all did poorly on the test."

   Teacher: "You mean you all did a bad job?"

   Pupil: "Yes."

   Yes_____ No_____

2. Pupil: "I'm confused about these problems."

   Teacher: "Do you mean you don't know how to 'borrow' when you are working on a subtraction problem or that you don't know which ones to do?"

   Pupil: "I don't know how to 'borrow' or 'carry.'"

   Yes_____ No_____

3. Pupil: "We sure get a bad deal on school dances."

   Teacher: "Do you mean that they cost too much, or they're not long enough, or do you feel we teachers aren't being fair?"

   Pupil: "No, I mean more kids would like coming to school if we had more dances."

   Yes_____ No_____

4. Pupil: "The Japanese people are very polite."

   Teacher: "Why do you say that?"

   Pupil: "They bow when they are introduced."

   Yes_____ No_____

5. Pupil: "The Indians were grossly mistreated by the whites."

TUNING IN ON LANGUAGE

Teacher: "In what way were they mistreated?"

Pupil: "Their land was taken from them."

Yes_____ No_____

Answers and Explanations

_____No_____ 1. The teacher is merely saying the same thing with different words at the same level of abstraction. One cannot be sure what is meant by "did poorly" or "did a bad job." The paraphrase needs to give two or more examples and avoid inferential-judgmental words like *bad*.

_____Yes_____ 2. In this case the teacher has given two examples using report words to show what the speaker's statement meant to him, and asked if this was the intended meaning.

_____Yes_____ 3. In this case three specific examples have been given, with a request to determine if any illustrate the intended meaning.

_____No_____ 4. This is not paraphrasing. The teacher is asking the student to explain why he said what he did. The teacher is not revealing her understanding of what the pupil has said.

_____No_____ 5. The teacher is not paraphrasing. He is asking the student for examples of what she meant. To paraphrase, the teacher would have to give two or more examples and ask if any were the intended meaning.

Directions

Again, identify which of the items below contain the behavior *paraphrasing.* If the example contains the behavior, check *yes.* If not, check *no.*

1. Pupil: "I hate spelling."

    Teacher: "Do you mean you don't like to write each word in a sentence?"

    Pupil: "Yes, and I don't like to memorize them either."

    Yes_____ No_____

2. Pupil: "This school just has too many rules."

    Teacher: "Do you mean we should do away with the rules of lining up after recess and no running in the halls?"

    Pupil: "Yes, and also the one of walking in lines in the halls."

    Yes_____ No_____

3. Pupil: "The pressure of the gas in the flask corresponds to the amount of heat we apply."

Teacher: "Are you saying that there is a positive correlation between pressure and temperature?"

Pupil: "Yes, that's right."

Yes_____ No_____

4. Pupil: "I think kids would accept more responsibility for the school if they were recognized as human beings."

Teacher: "Do you mean that you think students don't have an opportunity to have their ideas considered by the faculty and administration?"

Pupil: "Yes, the principal runs the student council, not the kids."

Yes_____ No_____

5. Pupil: "My daddy doesn't like dogs."

Teacher: "He won't get you a dog, or does he say he doesn't like dogs?"

Pupil: "He says they might bite me."

Yes_____ No_____

Answers and Explanations

___Yes___ 1. If you checked this as "no" because the teacher gave only one example, you are correct in that sense. It would be a better paraphrase if two or more examples had been given. However, you won't *always* be able to think of two examples—and, in this case, the teacher did give an example using report words and asked if that was the intended meaning.

___Yes___ 2. This does give two examples and asks if either is the intended meaning.

___No___ 3. This is word swapping at the same level of abstraction. To be a paraphrase, the teacher's statement would have to be an example using words with commonly agreed-on meanings, for example, "Are you saying that the more heat we apply, the more pressure there will be in the flask?"

___Yes___ 4. The teacher has given an example of what she thinks the student has intended to convey, and has asked if this is accurate. Of course, it would be a better paraphrase if the words were closer to report language and if more than one example had been given.

___Yes___ 5. The teacher is testing with specific examples to see if the meaning received is what the student intended.

TUNING IN ON LANGUAGE

ACTIVITIES: LEARNING TO PARAPHRASE

1. Write two examples of a teacher's paraphrase of a student's statement. Be prepared to share your examples with other members of the class.

2. Engage a personal friend in conversation for the express purpose of practicing the technique of *paraphrasing*. (If possible, tape-record the discussion.) After the discussion, recall the conversation as accurately as possible (or listen to the tape) and identify those instances in which you purposely paraphrased in order to probe for personal meaning. Then write an example from your conversation that you feel is an accurate illustration of the technique. Be prepared to share your example with other class members.

Asking for Illustrations

Often, in the communication process, it appears that the speaker could clarify meaning by offering illustrations. Asking the speaker to give illustrations lets her or him know that you think clarification would be helpful, perhaps because you are not sure *you* understand her or him or because you believe thinking about possible illustrations will help the speaker become more clear about what she or he is trying to say. To illustrate is to describe instances or give examples to create a more concrete image of what is meant. For example:

Pupil: **"It was more fun to be an explorer in the old days."**

Teacher: **"Tell me some things explorers did in the old days that made it more fun than now."**

Pupil: **"Well, like Columbus, when he landed in America, he didn't know what he would find. But the astronauts, when they landed on the moon, they already knew a lot about what it would be like."**

In this example the teacher's statement asked the pupil to give a specific illustration by saying, "Tell me some things explorers did. . . ."

Now look at another interaction:

Pupil: **"It was more fun to be an explorer in the old days."**

Teacher: **"What do you mean by that?"**

Pupil: **"It was more exciting."**

The teacher's statement in this example does not demonstrate the behavior of asking for illustrations. It sought clarification without indicating that examples or illustrative descriptions were the kind of clarification desired. Of course, the teacher may have had a good reason for asking, "What do you mean by that?" But we are looking for statements that *ask for illustrations.*

Here is another example:

Pupil: **"It was more fun to be an explorer in the old days."**

Teacher: **"That's an interesting idea."**

Pupil: **"When Columbus sailed across the ocean, he faced storms and mutiny, but the astronauts just sat quietly on their trip to the moon."**

Does the teacher's statement exemplify the behavior *asks for illustrations?* No. However, the pupil did give illustrations even though the teacher's statement was simply a comment on the idea expressed. Here, again, the statement may have been suitable to the teacher's intent of that moment, and may be the most effective technique with that pupil. The point for us is to identify the behavior *asks for illustrations* in the teacher's statement and not by looking at whether the pupil's response includes illustrations.

Here is another example:

Pupil: **"The Plains Indians depended on the buffalo."**

Teacher: **"In what ways did they depend on the buffalo?"**

Pupil: **"They used the skins for tepees. They ate the meat. Sometimes they used the bones for tools."**

In this case, the teacher has asked for a specific example or illustration.

EXERCISES: LEARNING TO ASK FOR ILLUSTRATIONS

Directions

Identify which of the examples contain the behavior *asks for illustrations.* If the example contains the behavior, check *yes.* If not, check *no.*

1.   Pupil: "Argentina's economy is based on the level of technology and beef production."

Teacher: "Would you repeat that?"

Pupil: "Argentina's economy is effected by the technical development of their factories."

                                                              Yes_____   No_____

2.   Pupil: "Argentina's economy is based on the level of technology and beef production."

Teacher: "What do you mean by level of technology?"

Pupil: "How modern their beef production plants are."

Yes_____ No_____

3. Pupil: "The Indians were deprived of their rights."

Teacher: "In what ways were they deprived of their rights?"

Pupil: "Well, their land was taken away from them."

Yes_____ No_____

4. Pupil: "Horses are very mean animals."

Teacher: "Why do you say that?"

Pupil: "I've seen horses kick other horses."

Yes_____ No_____.

5. Pupil: "If water came to the desert, manufacturing of some industrial products would increase."

Teacher: "What products do you have in mind?"

Pupil: "Farm machinery."

Yes_____ No_____

Answers and Explanations

_No_ 1. The teacher is asking for the message to be repeated. The request is not for an illustration or an example of what the student said.

_No_ 2. When the teacher asks for the student's meaning of a word or phrase, the student may respond with an illustration, but the question "What do you mean by _____?" may result in clarification of the term in a variety of ways, none of which would necessarily give an illustration.

Yes 3. This teacher's question definitely calls for illustrations. "In what ways were they deprived of their rights?" calls for specific examples.

_No_ 4. The teacher is not asking for an illustration or an example. She is only asking for an explanation of "why" the student said "Horses are mean." The fact that the student gave an example in this case is beside the point. He could very well have responded with, "My uncle says they are mean."

Yes 5. This one fits. It asks for specific examples or illustrations of the industrial products that the student thinks would increase.

Directions

Again, identify which of the examples below contain the behavior _asks for illustrations._ If the example contains the behavior, check _yes._ If not, check _no._

1. Pupil: "Eskimos are very rugged people."

   Teacher: "In what way?"

   Pupil: "They live for long periods of time out on the ice."

   Yes_____ No_____

2. Pupil: "School boards often inadvertently weaken the education program when they intend to strengthen it."

   Teacher: "What do you mean by that?"

   Pupil: "They sometimes use money for athletics when they need more teachers."

   Yes_____ No_____

3. Pupil: "Police officers are good."

   Teacher: "Oh? How are they good?"

   Pupil: "They help us across busy streets."

   Yes_____ No_____

4. Pupil: "There are many factors that control animal populations."

   Teacher: "What factors do you have in mind?"

   Pupil: "Abundance of food, population density, and adaptation to environment."

   Yes_____ No_____

5. Pupil: "Reading groups benefit the teacher, but they rarely benefit the kids."

   Teacher: "What leads you to make a statement like that?"

   Pupil: "It makes it easy for the teacher to manage the classroom, but kids in the low or buzzard group always feel unequal."

   Yes_____ No_____

Answers and Explanations

_____Yes__ 1. The question "In what way" asks for illustrations or examples of how the Eskimos are rugged people.

_____No__ 2. Asking, "What do you mean" may result in an illustration, as it did here; however, it could also have resulted in a response like, "School boards are often uninformed." The teacher hasn't asked for descriptions or illustrations of what was said.

_____Yes__ 3. The teacher has asked for a specific example.

_____Yes_ 4.   The teacher has asked for specific examples of factors.

_____No_ 5.   In this case, the teacher's response has resulted in an illustration although the teacher did not ask for illustrations. The teacher asked for the thought or observation behind the statement.

ACTIVITIES: ASKING FOR ILLUSTRATIONS

1.   Write two examples of a teacher *asking for illustrations*. Be prepared to share your examples with other members of the class.

2.   Engage a personal friend in conversation for the express purpose of practicing the technique of *asking for illustrations*. (If possible, tape-record the discussion.) After the discussion, recall the conversation as accurately as possible (or listen to the tape) and identify those instances in which you purposely asked for an illustration to clarify personal meaning. Then write an example from your conversation that you feel is an accurate illustration of the technique. Be prepared to share your example with other members of the class.

Note

This concludes Chapter 2, Tuning In on Language. You have not been asked to demonstrate the skills presented in this chapter in a teaching situation at this time. However, as you proceed through subsequent chapters, increasing emphasis will be placed on your ability to determine the personal meanings that students have for the words they use. Consequently, you are urged to practice the techniques at every available opportunity. The process may feel quite mechanical and artificial at first, but the key is "sincerity." Really *try* to understand the meanings that students have for those words that come across as ambiguous, inferential, or judgmental. The more you work at really trying to tune in on their meanings, the easier and more natural these tuning-in strategies will become.

Source Notes

1.   Hans Guggenheim, "The Concept of Culture," in *Man: A Course of Study; Talks to Teachers* (Cambridge, Mass.: Education Development Center, 1969), p. 39.
2.   Neil Postman and Charles Weingartner, *Teaching as a Subversive Activity* (New York: Delacorte Press, 1969), pp. xi–xiii.
3.   S.I. Hayakawa, *Language in Thought and Action* (New York: Harcourt, Brace, 1949), p. 31.
4.   Ibid., p. 32.

3 *Language Actions*

Overview

Rationale

The strategies for implementing the instructional process of inquiry are dependent on the teacher's ability to design and conduct discussions where students can generate and test their own ideas of what is "true," or "right," or "good." There are several taxonomies of intellectual processes that teachers can use to provide a structure for inquiry strategies. However, they have largely proven inadequate in the classroom. This chapter is based on a new and unique system for classifying intellectual processes that is evident in the language that people use when speaking.

General Objectives

At the conclusion of this chapter, you will have developed:

- An understanding of the rationale for categorizing questions and statements as language actions.

- The ability to discriminate and classify questions and statements according to the language action categories of *describing, explaining, predicting, choosing,* and *directing.*

- The ability to conduct a classroom discussion in which students are called on to respond in each of the language action categories.

Language Actions: Intellectual Processes for Developing Meaning

Treading the Treadmill of Trends

A fundamental characteristic of American education has been national trends, or ideas, techniques, or programs that have caught the imagination of teachers and administrators and have generated a great deal of hope for positive change. Most of the trends have involved the organization of materials and methods of delivering subject matter to students, for example, textbooks, educational films, programmed texts, "teacher proof" programs, departmentalized schools, platoon systems, homerooms, core programs, team teaching, individualized instruction, and open space. Trends have come and gone and repeated themselves. However, until recently, regardless of how many "revolutionary" ideas came and went, one phenomenon remained constant—the *process* of teaching. Teaching remained a process based on the belief that the teacher's role is to *impart* information and the student's role is to *acquire* information. Thus the teacher and the textbook (in whatever form) are *authorities*. They are the sources of knowledge and the judges of knowledge. The teacher and the textbook determine what is right or wrong, good or bad, acceptable or unacceptable. Students were made to feel that they were either successful, worthy persons or unworthy failures depending on the degree to which they could remember the "things" told to them by the teacher and/or the "things" read from the textbook. The inductive process of generating and testing ideas was simply not a part of most formal classroom experiences.

Only recently have systematic methods for examining teaching from the perspective of higher cognitive goals been available for those teachers who wish to break this pattern and change their role from that of imparters and judges of information to facilitators of information processing. In the past decade, research efforts have focused on the intellectual processing of information and the application of those processes to subject matter content. It is not my intent to present recent "process oriented" research activities in detail; however, a brief overview of three programs that have been especially useful as bases for the design of curricular and instructional systems will help you understand the rationale for the *language action classification system* presented in this text.

Bloom's Taxonomy of Educational Objectives

Benjamin Bloom's work has unquestionably had the greatest influence on the development of curricular programs and related teaching strategies for developing high-level cognitive processes. Bloom worked with a number of highly skilled and knowledgeable educators to arrive at the taxonomy of cognitive objectives. The taxonomy is presented in sequential and hierarchical form, defining precisely each stage or level of intellectual cognitive process and providing specific examples from a number of content fields to illustrate its application. Using this taxonomy as a guide, it is possible to analyze, define, and design goals to achieve specific cognitive processes at any level, in any subject matter area.

Condensed Version of Bloom's Taxonomy of Educational Objectives[1]

1.00 **Knowledge**
The recall of specifics and universals, methods and procedures, and pattern structures or settings.
   1.10 *Knowledge of Specifics*
   The recall of specific and isolable bits of information.
      1.11 *Knowledge of Terminology*
      Referents for specific symbols.
      1.12 *Knowledge of Specific Facts*
      Dates, events, persons, places, etc.

1.20 *Knowledge of Ways and Means of Dealing with Specifics*
    1.21 *Knowledge of Conventions*
        Ways of treating and presenting ideas and phenomena.
    1.22 *Knowledge of Trends and Sequences*
        Processes, directions, and movements of phenomena with respect to time.
    1.23 *Knowledge of Classification and Categories*
        Classes, sets, divisions, and arrangements for a given subject field.
    1.24 *Knowledge of Criteria*
        Criteria by which facts, principles, opinions, and conduct are tested or judged.
    1.25 *Knowledge of Methodology*
        Methods of inquiry, techniques, and procedures in a particular field.
1.30 *Knowledge of the Universals and Abstractions in a Field*
    Major schemes and patterns by which phenomena and ideas are organized.
    1.31 *Knowledge of Principles and Generalizations*
        Particular abstractions that summarize observations of phenomena.
    1.32 *Knowledge of Theories and Structures*
        Principles, generalizations, and interrelations that present a clear, rounded, and systematic view of a complex phenomenon, problem, or field.

2.00 **Comprehension**
    2.10 *Translation*
        Communication is changed (translated) from one form to another.
    2.20 *Interpretation*
        Explanation or summarization of a communication.
    2.30 *Extrapolation*
        Extension of trends or tendencies beyond the given data to determine implications, consequences, corollaries, effects, etc.

3.00 **Application**
    Use of abstractions (ideas) in particular and concrete situations.

4.00 **Analysis**
    Breakdown of a communication into its constituent elements or parts so that the relative hierarchy of ideas is made clear and/or relations between the ideas expressed are made explicit.
    4.10 *Analysis of Elements*
        Identification of the elements included in a communication.
    4.20 *Analysis of Relationships*
        Connections and interactions between elements and parts of a communication are identified.

4.30 *Analysis of Organizational Principles*
Organization, systematic arrangement, and structure that holds the communication together are identified.

5.00 **Synthesis**
Putting together elements and parts to form a whole.
5.10 *Production of a Unique Communication*
Development of a communication in which the writer or speaker attempts to convey ideas, feelings, and/or experiences to others.
5.20 *Production of a Plan or Proposed Set of Operations*
Development of a plan of work or the proposal of a plan of operations.
5.30 *Derivation of a Set of Abstract Relations*
Development of a unique set of abstract relations to classify or explain particular data or phenomena.

6.00 **Evaluation**
Judgments about the value of material and methods for given purposes.
6.10 *Judgments in Terms of Internal Criteria*
Evaluation of the accuracy of a communication based on personal criteria.
6.20 *Judgments in Terms of External Criteria*
Evaluation of material according to selected or remembered external criteria.

A survey of curriculum projects produced during the past several years shows clearly that Bloom's taxonomy has served as the underlying structure for sequencing subject matter content and designing many related instructional processes. Thus it has had a significant effect on classroom instruction. However, its inclusiveness makes it difficult to use as a basis for discussion strategies that facilitate the inquiry process of generating and testing knowledge. The strategies needed for implementing the inquiry process are clearly evident in the taxonomy, but it seems almost impossible for a teacher to master the taxonomy to the point of being able to sense immediately what level and process is being illustrated by what a student is saying at the time she or he is saying it. For example, suppose a third-grade class is discussing their trip to a lumberyard, and a student states, "I thought they would only sell things made of wood, but they don't. They sell everything you need to build a house." Or suppose a tenth-grade class is discussing the 1976 presidential debates and a student says, "If a candidate doesn't know too much about some important issues, it's better for him to avoid such national exposure."

In both cases, the appropriate response by the teacher is to help the students test the usefulness of their ideas. But if the teacher must first analyze the students' comments to determine if they are at the level of comprehension-interpretation, or analysis-relationships, or whatever specific classification, chances are good that the discussion will come to a quick and not very exciting conclusion. A far simpler taxonomy of intellectual processes is needed if the teacher is to respond quickly, naturally, and appropriately to the intellectual level of a student's comment.

Sanders' Classroom Questions

Norris Sanders' translation of Bloom's *Taxonomy of Educational Objectives* into a simplified taxonomy of classroom questions has proven to be extremely helpful to teachers in designing instruction. Sanders provides specific illustrations and presents a base of theory to support the use of questions in each of the following classifications.[2]

A Simplified Version of Sanders' Taxonomy of Questions

Memory

Facts ("What shape are Navajo houses?")

Definitions, Generalizations, and Values ("What kind of a man did the book say Socrates was?")

Skills ("What type of records of an event are most reliable?")

Translation Usually given in the form of a direction. ("Now put it in your own words.")

Interpretation

Comparative Relationship ("How are they different?")

Relationship of Implication ("How might the authors interpret the figures to support their own case?")

Relationship of an Inductive Generalization to Supporting Evidence ("What evidence is given to support the idea that great civilizations have not developed in the tropics?")

Relationship of a Value, Skill, or Definition to an Example of Its Use ("Compare the current foreign policy of the Soviet Union with that of the Republic of China.")

Quantitative Relationship ("Make a graph that shows each person's share of the national debt during each year from 1945 to 1963.")

Cause-and-Effect Relationship ("Why does the bimetallic blade always bend in the same direction?")

Application ("Based on our study of nutrition, how might we improve the menu for the school cafeteria?")

Analysis ("Tell why the reasoning in the following quotation is sound or unsound.")

Synthesis ("Devise a plan to determine whether students who salute the flag each day in school are more patriotic than those who do not have this experience.")

Evaluation ("Of the ten people listed, which five would you exclude from the bomb shelter?")

Sanders' text is an especially helpful, useful guide for designing questions. Although, like Bloom's taxonomy, the hierarchical sequence presented is too detailed for most of us to be able to analyze interaction *as* it occurs and respond appropriately at that moment, it is very helpful for designing questions in advance of instruction.

Guilford's Model of the Intellect

A third project that has had a very positive effect on curriculum design and instructional processes has been J. P. Guilford's research. Guilford conducted a factor analysis of known elements in the area of intellectual testing and measurement to construct a three-dimensional theoretical model of the structure of intelligence which encompasses (1) cognitive operations (intellectual processes), (2) the contents on which they operate, and (3) the product of the operations (see Chart 3-1).[3]

A Simplified Version of Guilford's Structure of the Intellect

Operations Major kinds of intellectual activities or processes (things the organism does with information).

Cognitive Memory   Simple reproduction of fact through recognition, rote memory, or recall. ("When was America discovered?")

Convergent Thinking   Analysis and integration of given or remembered data. Leads to one expected end result or answer. ("What transportation problems do large cities have in common?")

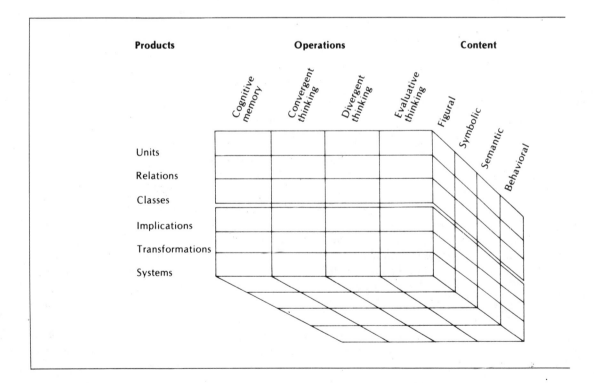

Divergent Thinking Intellectual operations wherein the individual is free to generate ideas independently of the data. ("What uses can be made of a brick?") ("What would life be like today if Germany had won World War II?") ("What would happen if water came to the desert?")

Evaluative Thinking Thinking dealing with value and choice characterized by judgmental quality. ("Who was the stronger president, Jackson or Jefferson?")

Content General varieties of information.

Figural Information in concrete form as perceived, conveying no intrinsic meaning. (Concrete objects.)

Symbolic Information in the form of signs, without significance in themselves but conveying meaning. (Letters, numbers, musical notations, etc.)

Semantic Information whose form of meaning is related to written and spoken language. (Words in written and spoken form.)

Behavioral Nonverbal information. (Gestures, facial expressions, bodily movements, etc.)

Products Results of the organism's processing of information.

Units Segregated or circumscribed items of information having "thing" character. (Apples, oranges, bricks, etc.)

Classes Aggregates of items of information grouped because of their common properties. (Fruit, cars, Caucasians, etc.)

Relations Recognized connections between units of information based on variables that apply to them. (Speed is dependent on technology.)

Implications Extrapolations of information in the form of expectancies, predictions, and consequences. (If the wind blows much harder, the roof will be torn off.)

Transformations Changes in existing or known information or in its uses. (A brick can be used for a bookend.)

Systems Organized or structured aggregates of items of information, interrelated and/or interacting. (Prices are fixed as a result of the amount of production and consumer desire.)

Guilford's model of the intellect is very useful for developing curriculum and designing instructional strategies. The categories are precise enough to effectively describe content, process, and products. The operations dimension is useful as a basis for designing questions for the inquiry process, and, in fact, can be used as a theoretical basis for supporting the classification system of an inquiry program. However, the total model, like Bloom and Sanders' taxonomies, is too inclusive to be used efficiently and effectively in conducting an inquiry discussion.

Rationale for a New System

While the advances described above have proven extremely valuable for researchers, curriculum developers, and instructional designers, and have served as a basis for several instructional systems,[4] they have been relatively ineffectual as guides for classroom teachers who wish to facilitate inquiry discussions. The inductive inquiry process is a logical, sequential, and cumulative process of acquiring and analyzing data, then generating ideas, and then testing ideas. What is needed is a model that (1) speaks directly to this process, (2) is inclusive enough to encompass the basic theoretical and instructional components of this process, and (3) is *simple enough* to become an *integrated, internalized,* and *natural* part of the teacher's behavior. For the inquiry process to be effective, the teacher must be able to function *spontaneously* and *naturally* in response to verbal and nonverbal student statements. The teacher must be accurately aware of the cognitive level of the statements and must be able to implement strategies that logically facilitate the building of meaning. The language actions classification system presented in this program is designed to satisfy these three criteria.

Language Actions: A Simplified Taxonomy That Works

The Northwest Regional Educational Laboratory has as a major purpose the design, development, and dissemination of instructional systems to improve teaching competence. This effort has produced three effective systems that help develop the understanding and skill to facilitate the processing of information by children. They are:

1. *The development of higher-level thinking abilities.*[5] This system is based on Hilda Taba's work which views the inductive teaching process as taking place in three phases: concept formation, interpretation of data, and application of knowledge.

2. *Facilitating inquiry in the classroom.*[6] This system is derived from the work of Richard Suchman and Ben Strasser who facilitated a process for keying teaching strategy to the data-generating and theorizing actions of students.

3. *Questioning strategies.*[7] This system is based on the work of James Gallagher which relates questions to Guilford's model of the intellect.

During the early 1970's, the authors of these programs began the process of designing a new system to synthesize the intellectual operations of the three systems. Their fundamental premise was that human beings do not have to be *taught* how to think, that thinking is a natural process of living. Logically then, this process of thinking should be evident in the language that people use. The words people use to talk about the issues, problems, and concerns of their life experiences should be symbolic of the thought processes used to deal with these issues, problems, and concerns. Also, the language used should contain words that have come to mean to most people what those thought processes are. It should not be necessary to invent new symbols or words to name these processes.

With this organizational theory, they quickly discovered that ordinary classroom speech can be classified into five categories. The five words commonly used to symbolize those processes are: *describing, explaining, predicting, choosing,* and *directing.* These categories denote and distinguish the following subprocesses in the process of generating and testing knowledge:

1. Making observations of a field of data. *Describing* the unique characteristics of a person, place, thing, event, phenomenon, or inner state.

2. Developing logical cause-and-effect relationships between sets of observations. *Explaining* the solution to a puzzle or a discrepancy. Stating the relationship between cause and effect.

3. Applying known cause-and-effect relationships to future events to generate probability statements. *Predicting* the probable consequences of a future event on the basis of existing ideas.

4. Analyzing alternatives and making a personal judgment based on either internal or external criteria. *Choosing* from alternatives.

The relationship of these four intellectual positions to other models and taxonomies for classifying cognitive processes is evident in the language of questions posed in each style.

Describing (sometimes called *memory* or *recall*): "What did you see, hear, read, feel, etc.?"

Explaining (sometimes called *interpretation* or *convergent thinking*): "Why did it . . . ? What caused it . . . ?"

Predicting (sometimes called *applying* or *divergent thinking*): "So what . . . ? What do you think would happen if . . . ?"

Choosing (sometimes called *evaluation* or *evaluative thinking* or *valuing*): "What do you believe? What would you prefer?"

The term *directing* is used to classify language statements that are in the form of imperative commands designed to cause someone to take action. As a language action, directing is treated somewhat separately in this system because its special function in the inquiry process is related more to curriculum design than it is to discussion strategies.

A teacher can become very proficient in using this classification system to design and implement strategies that cause students to generate and test knowledge for themselves. The following materials are designed to help you develop the ability to discriminate these language actions in the statements and questions of teachers and students. The materials are *not* designed to help you develop the understanding and skills to implement the inquiry process. The laboratory experience at the conclusion of this unit is simply for the purpose of practicing the use of the language actions classification system. The theoretical understandings and specific teaching behaviors for implementing the inquiry process are presented in Chapter 4, Interpreting.

Identifying Language Actions

When someone is talking, her or his statements and questions are in the form of language actions which may be categorized as describing, explaining, predicting, choosing, and directing. These language actions are the processes by which knowledge is generated and tested. The person describes available data, generates explanations of the world based on the data, and tests the explanations by predicting the future based on the explanations. Finally, choices are made, based on the understanding that has been generated. Directing is the imperative command to perform an action or function. The development of sensitivity to these language actions and the ability to discriminate among them provides a great deal of power in the determination and expression of meaning through language. The following activities are designed to develop this sensitivity and skill.

Describing (Observation, Memory, and Recall)

The meaning given here to the term *describing* is: A language action that either asks for or gives an observation of the distinctive characteristics of a person, place, thing, event, phenomenon, or inner state.

Describing requires no other thought process than selecting and combining words to report previously made or current observations of the characteristics of a person, place, thing, event, phenomenon, or inner state. For example:

"What is happening?" (Event)

"What is the address of the post office?" (Place)

"In what ways are Sue and Mary alike?" (Person)

"What are the steps in the scientific process listed in our book?" (Thing, recall of a specific point in a textbook)

"I was really tired last night." (Inner state)

"How do you feel about the Indochina situation?" (Inner state, asks for description of feeling)

"Tim said he didn't see the red light." (Person and event)

"What is the temperature of the room?" (Phenomenon)

In each of the above situations, the statement either asks for or gives an observation. It implies that one *knows* the distinctive characteristics of a person, place, thing, event, phenomenon, or inner state and can communicate them.

While a describing question calls for a verifiable observation to be given in report language, it is not uncommon for the response to be in the form of an inference or judgment. For example:

Question: **"What is life like in modern industrial Japan?"**
Response: **"Everyone is busy making transistor radios."** (Inference)

"The people are very polite and industrious." (Judgment)

Question: **"What was Cinderella's relationship to her stepmother?"**
Response: **"She hated her."** (Inference)
     "It was a crummy relationship." (Judgment)

Question: **"How do you feel?"**
Response: **"Lousy."** (Judgment)

In these cases, the response is still classified as *describing*. However, in order to determine precisely (in report language) what is meant by the inferential or judgmental terms, it is necessary to employ one of the techniques of "tuning in on personal meaning." (For example, "By lousy, do you mean sick to your stomach, or are you feeling depressed, or what?")

The primary difficulty in identifying the language action of describing is discriminating between *describing* and *explaining*. Consequently, before proceeding, let's examine the language action of explaining.

Explaining (Interpretation and Convergent Thinking)

The meaning given to the term *explaining* is: A language action that either asks for or gives the solution to a "puzzling phenomenon" or "discrepancy," of finding the relationship between cause and effect.

Explaining requires an intellectual process of acquiring information and formulating a logical cause-and-effect relationship between sets of observations. For example:

"What is there about the location of Portland that accounts for it being the largest city in Oregon?"

"Why is abundant rainfall important to Portland's economy?"

"What has been the effect of increasing interest rates on housing construction?"

"What caused the accident?"

"The increasing heat created a liquid state."

"I was able to get my car started by rolling it down the hill and using compression."

"Much of the health problems in _____ can be attributed to the extremely poor economic conditions."

"What you just said to Mary really makes me mad!"

In each of the above examples the person is either asking for or giving a logical cause-and-effect relationship between sets of observations. In the case of questions, there is a "gap" in understanding, a "puzzle," a discrepancy. The response fills in the gap, solves the puzzle, and accounts for the discrepancy. The essential characteristic of explaining, therefore, is one of stating the *cause-and-effect* relationship of one thing to another.

When the statement either gives or asks for a *reason for* or *effect of* something occurring, the word *because* is either explicitly or implicitly evident, demonstrating the cause-and-effect relationship. Something happens *because* of something else. For example:

"**Water in the gasoline** *caused* **the car to stall.**"

"**Providing coffee breaks** *resulted* **in a higher production ratio.**"

"**Increasing the heat** *produced* **a violent reaction.**"

"**Weatherproofing the windows** *helped* **lower heating costs.**"

"**The student's talking** *interfered* **with my train of thought.**"

Notice that all of the above statements can be considered as responses to antecedent questions asking why, what caused, how come, and what effect.

Question Form   Thus the cause-and-effect question is a form of: "What is the reason(s) for . . . ?" or "What is the effect(s) of . . . ?" The *question* asks for cause or effect.

"**What caused the car to stall?**"

"**How come the motor quit running?**"

"**Why did the car stop?**"

"**How do you account for the car stopping?**"

"**What happened when the gas cap was left off?**"

"**What was the consequence of leaving the gas cap off?**"

Statement Form   The cause-and-effect *statement* explicitly states the cause-and-effect relationship of one thing to another. For example: "Water in the gasoline" (observation 1) "caused" (relationship) "the car to stall" (observation 2). "Leaving the gas cap off" (observation 1) "resulted in" (relationship) "water getting into the gas" (observation 2) "which in turn caused" (relationship) "the car to stall" (observation 3). "I was able to obtain better mileage" (observation 1) "as a consequence of" (relationship) "using higher octane gasoline" (observation 2).

Describing vs. Explaining

It is sometimes difficult to discriminate between describing and explaining. A basic problem occurs because quite often the response to an explaining question is given in the form of a describing statement. For example, notice the relationship between the question and response in each of the following:

Question: **"Why did he have difficulty walking?"**
Response: **"The sidewalk was icy."**

Question: **"How did you get to the top of the hill?"**
Response: **"I used a rope."**

Question: **"What was the consequence of adding salt to the solution?"**
Response: **"The solution is now saline."**

In each case, the response, when taken out of the context of its antecedent question, is a describing statement, and would be categorized as describing. That is, the response is an observation.

However, if a teacher asks, "Why are some of the plants greener than others?" he is obviously asking for a causal relationship. If a student responds, "Some plants received more sun than others," she is indicating a causal relationship, regardless of whether or not she explicitly stated, "Some plants are greener than others because some received more sun than others."

Consequently, analysis of language actions should consider each statement in context. When a statement is an obvious and logical response to an antecedent *explaining question,* the statement should be categorized as *explaining* even though the statement, taken out of context, is describing.

Another problem in discriminating between explaining and describing is related to the common misuse of the term *explain.* It is quite common to use *explain* when the terms *tell* or *describe* should more properly and logically be used. For example: "Let me explain to you how I feel." "Explain where the post office is." "Explain what a light switch does." In each of these examples, the words *tell* or *describe* could be substituted for *explain* and would more effectively convey the meaning of the statement. Generally, one describes feelings, or tells how one feels; one describes or tells where a thing is located; and one describes or tells what something does. In such cases, where the statement either gives or asks for an observation of the unique characteristics of a person, place, thing, event, phenomenon, or inner state rather than the cause-and-effect relationship of one observation to another, the statement is classified as *describing* even though the term explain is explicitly evident.

Although this is not a discrimination problem, one should be aware that explanations are often asked for or given in a form that implies *speculation.* For example:

"Why did it explode?" might be asked as:

"Why do you *think* **it exploded?"** or
"Why do you *suppose* **it exploded?"** or
"Why do you *believe* **it exploded?"**

The words *think, suppose,* and *believe* all have a connotation of speculation and therefore can be confused with predicting. People generally use these terms as modifiers of the intellectual process called for. For example:

"Why do you *think* **it exploded?"** (Explaining)

"What do you *suppose* **will happen under the new President?"** (Predicting)

"What do you *believe* **is the best car?"** (Choosing)

Such words should not be considered as changing the basic intent of the question or answer.

EXERCISES: DISCRIMINATING BETWEEN DESCRIBING AND EXPLAINING

Directions

Discriminate between describing and explaining by identifying each of the items below. Code each item as either:

D—Describing, or

E—Explaining

_____ 1. "The development of steam power made railroads possible." (Response to "What effect did steam power have on the development of transportation?")

_____ 2. "Eskimos live in cold climates."

_____ 3. "What's causing that man to jump around and yell like that?"

_____ 4. "The difference between Hortense and Myrtle is that Myrtle thinks before she talks."

_____ 5. "Hitler missed his chance of invading England by picking the wrong time and the wrong place."

_____ 6. "Why do the Netsiliks build rock piles when hunting caribou?"

_____ 7. "Rock piles simulate men." (Response to question 6)

_____ 8. "The story says that he dug the Grand Canyon with his Blue Ox hitched to a plow."

_____ 9. "The reason that Ireland is called the Emerald Isle is that it is so green." (Response to "Why is Ireland called the Emerald Isle?")

_____10. "Would you like to explain to me where Washington School is located?"

Answers and Explanations

_____E_____ 1. This is *explaining* since it gives a cause-and-effect relationship in response to a question that clearly asks for an *effect*.

_____D_____ 2. This is an observation *describing* where Eskimos live.

_____E_____ 3. This is *explaining* since it asks the person to give the *cause* of the man's jumping and yelling.

_____D_____ 4. This is an observation *describing* the difference between two individuals.

_____D or E_____ 5. This is one of those difficult statements to discriminate. It could be simply *describing* a historical event. However, if the word *by* connotes *because of* or *as a result of,* it also connotes a cause-and-effect relationship and identifies the statement as *explaining.* If it is important to discriminate between whether the person is *describing* an observation or *explaining,* the only way of knowing is to ask for more information, for example, "Are you saying that the *cause* of Hitler's failing was . . . ?"

_____E_____ 6. This is asking for a cause-and-effect relationship.

_____E_____ 7. Although the statement "Rock piles simulate men" by itself is an observation and therefore *describing*, in this case it is a direct and logical response to an *explaining* question and must be considered in context as "Netsiliks build rock piles when hunting caribou *because* rock piles simulate men." Therefore the statement is scored as *explaining.*

_____D_____ 8. This is *describing* or telling what the story related.

_____E_____ 9. This is *explaining* by telling the *cause* of something, in response to a question asking for cause.

_____D_____ 10. This is *describing* from two points of reference. First, it asks if the person would like to do something. The anticipated response is, "Yes, I would" or "No, I wouldn't." Second, the word *explain* is misused here. To properly convey the intended meaning, the words *describe* or *tell* should be used.

Directions

Again, discriminate between the items listed below. Code each item as either:

D—Describing, or

E—Explaining

_____ 1. "What effect does smog have on the lungs?"

_____ 2. "Redheads often have freckles."

_____ 3. "The law of supply and demand largely determines the price of apples."

_____ 4. "He was looking for someone with a red carnation in his lapel."

_____ 5. "How does the rudder of an airplane function in flight?"

_____ 6. "In what ways were the boat-building practices of the Mediterranean cultures like those of the Nordic tribes?"

_____ 7. "How did the development of steam power make railroads possible?"

_____ 8. "The steam engine was the first portable, economically efficient, and powerful engine." (Response to question 7)

_____ 9. "What did our book list as the three main reasons for the French Revolution?"

_____ 10. "Desire for liberty, desire for equality, and fraternity within the lower classes." (Response to question 9)

Answers and Explanations

___E___ 1. Cause-effect relationship. It asks for the *effect* of one thing.

___D___ 2. Observation. This *describes* redheads.

___E___ 3. Cause-effect relationship. This tells the probable *cause* of something.

___D___ 4. Observation. This *describes* what a person did.

___E___ 5. This asks for the *function* or *effect* of one thing on another. It calls for an *explanation* of how the rudder affects the flight pattern.

___D___ 6. This asks for a noncausal comparative relationship. The person is asked to *describe* practices of the two cultures.

___E___ 7. Cause-effect relationship. This asks, "What *effect* did steam power have on the development of the railroads?"

___E___ 8. This statement, taken out of the context of the antecedent question, is *describing*. However, in this case, the response is a logical response to a request for a cause-and-effect relationship. Therefore it is scored as *explaining*.

___D___ 9. If the question had asked, "What were the reasons or *causes* of the French Revolution?" it would be asking for a cause-and-effect relationship. But in this case, the question simply asks the respondent to *describe* or tell what the book listed. It asks for an observation of what the book stated.

___D___ 10. Observation. This *describes* what the book said.

Note

Although this chapter is not designed to present the teaching behaviors necessary to implement the inquiry process, it is important to realize that the language action of *explaining* is the intellectual process of *generating knowledge*, generating solutions to problems. Therefore it is essential that you develop the skill to identify quickly and accurately cause-and-effect relationships in questions and statements.

Predicting (Extrapolation and Divergent Thinking)

The meaning given here to the term *predicting* is: A language action that either asks for or gives the future consequences of an action, event, or circumstance.

Predicting requires an intellectual process of speculating about probable results of applying ideas and information to future events. For example:

"What will happen if we add acid to the solution?"

"What do you think would be the effect of completely eliminating any form of arbitrary grading system from the public schools?"

"What would happen if all the food a person needs were reduced to just one pill a day?"

"Juvenile delinquency could be considerably reduced if more money was available for education."

"I feel we could improve our image with the world if we would stop buying political favors with military aid."

"If we doubled the tax on gasoline and used that money for antipollution research, we could go a long way toward solving our ecology problems."

In each of these examples, the speaker is either asking for or giving hypotheses in relation to a future situation. That is, predictions of what *might* happen are being asked for or given.

Predicting is a basic "testing" process of knowledge building and testing. It is applying known or suspected cause-and-effect relationships to a future event. For example, if I have developed the explanation (theory or hypothesis) that "Failures in my class are caused by the letter grading system," I can test the usefulness of that idea by predicting: "If I eliminate the letter grading system and maintain the same content and processes, I will have fewer failures."

At this point we need not be concerned about whether data are immediately available to test or verify the validity of a prediction. It is obvious that some predictions are in the realm of fantasy (for example, "What would happen if all the food a person needs were reduced to just one pill a day?"); some are immediately testable (for example, "What will happen if we add acid to the solution?"); and some can be tested over a period of time (for example, "Fewer failures will result if letter grades are eliminated."). In the next chapter, considerable emphasis is placed on developing an awareness of the differences in the testability of predictive statements. Right now, though, the task is to develop the skill to discriminate the language action of *predicting* in questions and statements. Basically, the key is: Does the statement *ask for or give probable future consequences of an action, event, or circumstance?*

EXERCISES: DISCRIMINATING AMONG DESCRIBING, EXPLAINING, AND PREDICTING

Directions

Discriminate among *describing, explaining,* and *predicting* by coding each item as one of these:

LANGUAGE ACTIONS

D—Describing

E—Explaining

P—Predicting

_____ 1. "Illegal strikes could be broken by calling in the National Guard."

_____ 2. "We could improve the postal service by charging more for stamps."

_____ 3. "The stock market improved as a result of the strike ending."

_____ 4. "If the strike were over, the stock market would improve."

_____ 5. "What do you think caused the strike?"

_____ 6. "Can you think of how we could avoid postal strikes in the future?"

_____ 7. "What caused the postal strike?"

_____ 8. "The President went on television and explained his reasons for calling in the National Guard."

_____ 9. "What are your feelings about the strike?"

_____10. "What might be the effect of calling in the National Guard?"

Answers and Explanations

__P__ 1. This is *predicting* since it speculates about a future consequence of calling in the National Guard. Notice that it does not say, "Illegal strikes can be broken by . . ." The term *could* is used, implying *"in the future."*

__P__ 2. Again, a *prediction*. We don't know, it hasn't been proven, so we're only *predicting* that postal services could be improved by charging more for stamps.

__E__ 3. This is an *explanation* of what happened. The stock market improved as a *result* of (by means of, as a consequence of, as an effect of) the strike ending.

__P__ 4. Again, we don't know this—it is a speculation about the unknown future. "What *would* happen?" "What do you *predict would* happen?"

__E__ 5. Did you code this as *predicting*? If you did it was probably because of the word *think*. It's a very ambiguous term that can imply speculation. However, in this case it seems pretty clear that you're being asked to speculate about the cause—"What do you think *caused* the strike?"

__P__ 6. Did you code this as *explaining*? If so, it's an easy and natural mistake to make. However, this calls for a *predicting* operation, even though it is presented in an inverted form; that is, the desired future condition is given (not asked for). Nevertheless, the causal conditions asked for can only be arrived at through a prediction process.

_____E_____ 7. This time this is clearly asking for a cause-and-effect relationship, not future but past. "What *caused* the strike?"

_____D_____ 8. Did the word *explained* catch you? *Told* or *described* is more appropriate since the statement simply *describes* what the President did, it says nothing about what his reasons were.

_____D_____ 9. *Describing* again. In this case the question asks for a *description* of feelings, for an observation of an inner state.

_____P_____ 10. Did the word *effect* mislead you into coding this as *explaining*? You are being asked to *predict* the future. "What *might* be the effect *if* you called in the National Guard?"

If you had difficulty discriminating the language action of *predicting*, go back and examine each item in relation to the following clue. Notice that all but one predicting statement not only relates to a future situation but also contains one of the following words: *would, could,* or *should.* For example:

"What *could* be done?"

"Services *could* be improved."

"What *would* happen?"

"The market *would* improve."

"How *should* we avoid it?"

This clue will not always be evident. The statement *might* be:

"What *will* happen?"

"Rain *will* fall if the conditions are right."

"What *might* result?"

But the clue is still helpful. The tentative nature of a *predicting* statement is very often expressed by the presence of the words could, would, or should.

Directions

Again, discriminate among *describing, explaining,* and *predicting* by coding each item D, E, or P.

_____ 1. "Why do you think the airlines are losing money?"

_____ 2. "One of the reasons Alaska has so few people is because the weather is so cold."

_____ 3. "If the present trends continue, it will be difficult to tell women from men."

_____ 4. "Hijackers should be given life sentences in the penitentiary."

_____ 5. "The cost of replacing hijacked airliners has resulted in higher fares for passengers."

_____ 6. "If the group would settle on just one problem, they could make a decision."

_____ 7. "Airline hijackers have cost the airlines a great deal of money."

_____ 8. "We could end wars by drafting politicians."

_____ 9. "What do you believe would be the effect of a death penalty for airline hijackers?"

_____10. "More teachers should run for public office if we ever expect to have sufficient money for schools."

Answers and Explanations

____E____ 1. There's that word *think* again. You are being asked to speculate, but to speculate as to the *reasons* or *causes* for the airlines losing money.

____E____ 2. This is an *explaining* statement of a cause-and-effect relationship.

____P____ 3. This *predicts* the future; it is a definite speculation as to what *will* happen.

____D____ 4. This is a *describing* statement that *describes* or *tells* how the speaker *feels* about hijackers. Although the word *should* is evident, there is nothing in the statement to indicate an "if-then" prediction.

____E____ 5. This gives a cause-and-effect relationship and is therefore *explaining*.

____P____ 6. This *predicts* a possible consequence of group action and is thus an "if-then" statement.

____D____ 7. This is a personal observation of a phenomenon and thus *describing*.

____P____ 8. This is a *prediction* that some people would like to test.

____P____ 9. This asks the person to predict what the *effect* of the death penalty would be. Also, it contains the ambiguous word *believe*: "What do you *believe* (speculate or predict) would be the *effect* of . . . (*future consequences of*).

____P____10. Unlike item 4, the word *should* in this item indicates the tentative nature of an "if-then" hypothesis or *prediction*.

Choosing (Evaluation, Evaluative Thinking, and Valuing)

The meaning given here to the term *choosing* is: A language action that either asks for or gives a choice between two or more alternatives.

Choosing is an intellectual process of analyzing alternatives and formulating personal judgments based on either internal or external criteria. Choosing is a process of "valuing" that answers the question, "Which of two or more alternatives do I value most highly?" For example:

"Do you consider golf, swimming, or jogging to be the best exercise for a middle-aged, overweight man like me?"

"Which of the Japanese import cars do you prefer?"

"What do you feel we should do — pull out of Indochina completely, give them more economic aid, or try to use military force to make them accept our form of government?"

"I like swimming as an exercise better than jogging."

"I prefer Datsun to any of the others that I've seen."

"I'd rather be a blonde than a brunette."

In each of the examples, the person is either asking for or giving a personal choice between two or more alternatives. The *choosing* action may be evident as a statement that indicates that one thing is preferred over others, or that one thing is more appropriate than other things, or that one thing is being selected over other things — that is, the action is a process of *choosing* from among alternatives.

We will not now explore in detail the intellectual or affective elements involved in the choosing action. Choosing is part of the valuing process by which individuals identify, analyze, select, and commit themselves to a value system, and is an extremely important part of the total teaching-learning process and an important part of testing ideas. Considerable attention will be directed to this process in Chapter 5. Here our concern is to develop the skill of discriminating the language action of choosing as it occurs in verbal interaction.

In order for *choosing* to occur, the alternatives for choice must be found in the words of the statement or must be unquestionably evident from the context of the interaction. For example, in the statement: "I prefer coffee to tea or milk," the speaker is stating (1) a preference and (2) the alternatives from which the choice was made. Consider the following dialogue:

Question: **"Do you want ham or turkey?"**

Response: **"I want ham."**

The first person is asking for choice and the second person is *choosing.* The statement "I want ham," taken by itself, is *describing* — the individual is *describing* a desire for ham. However, in this example, the statement "I want ham" is a *choosing* action because the alternative for choice is found in the antecedent question. Basically, the clues are:

1. Does the statement ask for or make a choice?

2. Are the alternatives for choice apparent or clearly inferrable from the statement or dialogue?

Directions

Discriminate among *describing, explaining, predicting,* and *choosing* by coding each item as:

D—Describing

E—Explaining

P—Predicting

C—Choosing

_____ 1. "I like chocolate ice cream better than vanilla or strawberry."

_____ 2. "How did the development of steam power make railroads possible?"

_____ 3. "It's better that men shoot for the moon than shoot at each other."

_____ 4. "If a teacher has a problem it would help to talk it over with the principal."

_____ 5. "Air pollution and water pollution both result in damage to life."

_____ 6. "Of all the problems that America has, air pollution is the worst."

_____ 7. "Which is the best highway to take to drive from Portland to San Francisco in the shortest time?"

_____ 8. "I value hard work more than play."

_____ 9. "My favorite Thursday night television program is Hawaii Five-O."

_____ 10. "What would happen if we spent more money on social welfare and less on defense?"

Answers and Explanations

___C___ 1. This is a definite *choosing* action. Both the choice and the alternatives for choice are clearly evident.

___E___ 2. This item asks for a cause-and-effect relationship and is thus *explaining.*

___C___ 3. The person is indicating a clear *choice* between two alternatives. The criteria for judgment are not evident, but a value is being expressed, which implies a definite choice: "Better shoot for the moon than at someone else."

___P___ 4. This is *predicting* in that it states a hypothesis relative to what *would* happen as a consequence of a certain action.

___E___ 5. This is a cause-and-effect relationship: "Pollution *causes* damage."

_C or D_ 6. If you coded this as either *choosing* or *describing*, your response is understandable. The statement could be a personal observation *describing* an inner state: how a person "feels" about air pollution. However, the person may be expressing a definite *choice*, with internal criteria for judging what she or he believes to be the worst problem of all the (limitless?) problems America faces today. The alternatives are not clearly evident but they are implied.

_C_ 7. You might not agree with this because alternatives are not clearly evident. However, if you wish to drive to San Francisco from Portland, the points of departure and destination imply a set of specific alternative routes.

_C_ 8. This clearly states that one thing is preferred over another. The person *chooses* to work.

_C or D_ 9. If you coded this as *choosing*, you are right. The choice is clear: "Hawaii Five-O." The implied alternatives are the other programs on Thursday evening. However, if you coded it as *describing*, you are also right. The person is clearly *describing* feelings. He or she *likes* "Hawaii Five-O" and is reporting this observation. (Another example of how the words do not always convey a speaker's intended meaning.)

_P_ 10. This is *predicting*, since the person is being asked to hypothesize about the consequences of a future action.

Directions

Again, discriminate among *describing*, *explaining*, *predicting*, and *choosing* by coding each item D, E, P, or C.

_____ 1. "I feel Lincoln was a better President than either Washington or Jefferson."

_____ 2. "Ultimately, men and women will dress the same and hold the same kinds of jobs if present trends continue."

_____ 3. "Are you more irritated by what Bill just said?"

_____ 4. "According to the physical education program we have, jogging is a good exercise."

_____ 5. "I'd sure as heck rather go skiing than fix a leaky faucet."

_____ 6. "Which of the four major West Coast cities do you feel would be the most enjoyable place to live?"

_____ 7. "Why didn't you come to the party?"

_____ 8. "I wasn't feeling well." (Response to question 7)

_____ 9. "Please explain to me the way to the bus depot from here."

_____ 10. "Which of these three ties do you think looks best with this suit?"

Answers and Explanations

_____C_____ 1. The individual has clearly chosen Lincoln as being better than the other two stated alternatives.

_____P_____ 2. The person is *predicting* the future, speculating about what she or he thinks will happen as a consequence of a trend.

_____D_____ 3. The person is being asked to *describe* or report on a personal observation of an inner state.

_____D_____ 4. No one is *choosing* jogging. The person is *describing* what the P.E. manual says.

_____C_____ 5. This statement clearly indicates a personal *choice* between two explicitly stated alternatives.

_____C_____ 6. There may be a question here as to what the speaker means by "major West Coast cities," but the alternatives are stated and the person is being asked to *choose* one.

_____E_____ 7. The question here asks for a cause-and-effect relationship, and is thus *explaining*.

_____E_____ 8. The response (which when taken by itself is *describing*) when considered in relation to the question is a logical response and is therefore coded *explaining*.

_____D_____ 9. Don't let the word *explain* fool you. *Describe* or *tell* is more appropriate to the intended meaning. The person is being asked to *describe* the route to the bus depot.

_____C_____ 10. This is clearly a case of being asked to choose one of three alternatives.

Directing

The meaning given here to the term *directing* is: A language action that clearly tells another to perform an action or function. For example:

"John, please close the door."

"Bluebirds, bring your readers to the circle. Buzzards, continue to work in your workbooks."

"Mary, tell us in your own words what the book says."

In each of these examples, the individual is telling someone to perform a particular action or function.

We are not concerned about the most effective way to give directions. The task now is to develop the ability to discriminate between statements that clearly tell an individual to perform an action or function and those that do not. The basic difficulty is that often an individual intends to direct another to perform a particular action or function, but phrases the statement in the form of a *describing, explaining, predicting,* or *choosing* action. For example:

"Please state your name." *(Directing)*

"Would you like to tell us your name?" *(Describing—"inner state")*

"What is your name?" *(Describing—thing)*

"I need your name so I'll know who to call." *(Explaining)*

"If you give me your name, I'll call on you." *(Predicting)*

"Would you tell us your name?" *(Choosing)*

The problem is not one of attempting to infer the teacher's intent—it is to classify the language action according to the words used. In the above statements, only the first is clearly *directing* the individual to perform an action or function. The other statements may or may not result in obtaining the person's name, but only the first is clearly *directing* the person to state his or her name.

EXERCISES: DISCRIMINATING AMONG DESCRIBING, EXPLAINING, PREDICTING, CHOOSING, AND DIRECTING

Directions

Discriminate among *describing, explaining, predicting, choosing,* and *directing* by coding each item:

> D—Describing
>
> E—Explaining
>
> P—Predicting
>
> C—Choosing
>
> DR—Directing

_____ 1. "Please close the window, Jim."

_____ 2. "Would you mind closing the window, Sue?"

_____ 3. "I'd like someone back there to close the window."

_____ 4. "Billy, close the window beside you, please."

_____ 5. "If someone would close that window, it would be much warmer in here."

_____ 6. "It's cold in here with that window open."

_____ 7. "Will you close the window, Mary?"

_____ 8. "That open window is causing this room to be awfully uncomfortable."

_____ 9. "Close the window now, Bill."

_____10. "Is there a draft in this room? I'm freezing!"

Answers and Explanations

___DR___ 1. "Please close the window, Jim" is a clear *direction* that tells the individual to perform a particular action.

___D___ 2. Sue is being asked if she "minds" closing the window, that is, she is being asked to *describe* her feelings. If you scored this as *choosing*, it's understandable, but wrong. The question is close to asking her if she *chooses* to close the window, but it actually asks her to report on how she feels about closing the window.

___D___ 3. This time the teacher is *describing* feelings: "I'd *like* someone to close the window."

___DR___ 4. Billy is being given a clear *direction:* "Billy, close the window beside you, please."

___P___ 5. The teacher is *predicting* or hypothesizing what would happen *if* the window were closed. (This is the kind of statement that is often resented by many individuals including this writer. It can easily be interpreted as an attempt to manipulate another person into doing something.)

___D or E___ 6. You probably coded this as *describing*, as a report giving an observation of an inner state of being cold. However, you could have logically coded it as *explaining*, as a cause-and-effect relationship: "It's cold in here with (as a consequence or effect of) that window open."

___C___ 7. This is giving the student a simple *choice*. "Will you (or won't you) close the window, Mary?"

___E___ 8. This is a cause-and-effect relationship, or *explaining:* "That open window is *causing* (resulting in) this room to be awfully uncomfortable."

___DR___ 9. This is a clear *direction* to perform an action.

___D___10. This is *describing*, since it both asks for an observation and gives an observation.

Again, the purpose here is not to imply the most effective way to manage or control the classroom. However, it should be obvious at this point that teachers should not be surprised or angered by students misinterpreting their intent as a result of the way in which their statements are worded.

Directions

Again, discriminate among *describing, explaining, predicting, choosing,* and *directing* by coding each item as D, E, P, C, or DR.

_____ 1. "Will the Jets please bring their workbooks and come to the circle?"

_____ 2. "I would like you to put your equipment away now."

_____ 3. "Put your crayons away now, please."

_____ 4. "If you work hard on this sheet, you will be able to go outside sooner."

_____ 5. "Would you like to get your math books out now, class?"

_____ 6. "Please get your math books out now, class."

_____ 7. "Taking so much time to get ready is causing us to be late for P.E."

_____ 8. "Will you kids settle down or not?"

_____ 9. "If that noise doesn't stop back there, someone's going to be in trouble!"

_____ 10. "Mary, explain to the class why the answer to this problem is 20 square feet."

Answers and Explanations

___C___ 1. This is giving the students a *choice:* "Will you (or won't you) bring your workbooks and come to the circle?" (The teacher shouldn't be surprised if at least one Jet chooses not to.)

___D___ 2. The teacher is *describing* feelings: "I would *like* you to put your equipment away."

___DR___ 3. No question here, the teacher is *directing* or telling the students to put their crayons away.

___P___ 4. If you coded this as *explaining,* it's understandable, but wrong. The teacher is *predicting* what will happen in the *future if* they hit the books. It may be a promise, but it's still *predicting* a future action.

___D___ 5. This is another one of those fine lines between *describing* and *choosing,* but the teacher is not asking "would you" or "would you not" (choice) "get your books out." The teacher is asking the students to describe their feelings: "Would you *like* to get your math books out?"

___DR___ 6. This is a clear *directing* statement: "Please get your math books out."

___E___ 7. The implication may be to "hustle it up," but the statement is a clear cause-and-effect relationship, or *explaining.*

___C___ 8. The teacher is giving them a clear *choice* between two alternatives: "Will you settle down or not?"

<u>   P   </u> 9. The teacher is *predicting* future consequences: "*If* that noise doesn't stop, *then* someone's going to be in trouble." (Threats really do invite kids to test them, don't they?)

<u> DR </u> 10. This is a clear *direction* to Mary to perform the language action of *explaining*. One might seriously question when and how such a direction as this might be given, but it is definitely a *direction* to perform an action.

Note

The next activity asks you to prepare to conduct a teaching experience in which you will read a story, newspaper article, or similar content source to students and then ask a series of questions to illustrate each of the language actions. If you are in a class, work in a group to prepare for this experience. Prior to the next session, find a story, newspaper article, or similar source of content focus you feel would be appropriate for the grade level of students with which you will be working. Take the material with you to the next session. If you are reading this text independently, find an appropriate source before proceeding.

ACTIVITIES: PREPARING FOR LABORATORY EXPERIENCE

The purpose of this exercise is to design a specific questioning sequence for conducting a laboratory experience with students in a classroom setting.

Directions

If you are a member of a class, meet in groups of three or four to proceed through the following steps to design a question sequence. If you are proceeding through the text independently, complete item 2 below. If possible, test your questions by role playing with one or more interested colleagues.

1. Indicate the grade level you intend to work with and read your chosen story or article to the other members of your group. If group members do not find the material appropriate for the age and interest level of the students, find new material before proceeding.

2. Cooperatively design a question sequence to be used in conducting a discussion.
    a. Initially, brainstorm questions. Record without criticism or discussion any questions that come to mind.
    b. Select and refine questions to be asked in the following order:
        Two or more questions asking students to *describe*.
        Two or more questions asking students to *explain*.
        One or more questions asking students to *predict*.
        One or more questions asking students to *choose*.

3. Role-play the discussion as a teacher and students. Try to anticipate as realistically as possible what the students might say in response to each question.

4. Revise and refine the questions until all members feel that they have an appropriate sequence for conducting the lab experience.

5. Review the following sequences: "Criteria for Success," "Procedure for Lab Experiences," and "Directions for Taping a Lesson."

Laboratory Experience: Criteria for Success

The objective of this chapter has been to develop the skill to design and ask questions that accurately demonstrate each of the language actions. Therefore the following criteria should be used in judging the level of competence demonstrated in a laboratory experience.

1. The questions accurately demonstrate the language action called for in each category of describing, explaining, predicting, and choosing.

2. All materials are ready in advance and are utilized in a planned, sequential manner as evident by the absence of management problems during the lesson.

The basic purpose of this lesson is to try the language classification system and assess your ability to use it accurately. It is also important for you to pay attention to whether you are accepting students' explanations without judging them right or wrong or good or bad. Also, try to avoid responding with such phrases as "Right!" and "Very good!" Try to substitute phrases such as "I see," "I understand," and "That's an interesting idea."

At the describing level make sure that the data being considered are accurate observations, for example, by stating, "Let's check that observation again."

Clarify terminology and ideas by asking for personal meaning, paraphrasing, and by asking for illustrations.

Give psychological support to students who seem to need it, for example, by saying such things as "Take your time," "Would you like to think about it for a few minutes?" "Mistakes are part of learning, aren't they?"

Procedure for Lab Experiences

If you are not now a teacher with your own group of students, the following suggestions will facilitate your effective, efficient arrangements for obtaining a group of students.

1. If you know a group of students available for conducting laboratory experiences, be certain to make arrangements well in advance with both the cooperating teacher and the principal. Follow the directions below for scheduling and conducting the lesson.

2. If you *do not* know of such a group of students, either your instructor will designate a school and teacher for you to contact, or you will need to contact a school and make arrangements personally.

3. Contact the principal first. Describe the program and request the opportunity to meet with a teacher of the appropriate grade level. (Emphasize that the content ordinarily taught in that class is not relevant. You simply need six to twelve students from any class.)

4. Contact the teacher and arrange for a personal conference. During the conference:
    a. Arrange with the teacher for the specific day, time, and location of the laboratory experience. You may wish to give the teacher a copy of Arrangements for Laboratory Experience.
    b. Discuss taping procedures. Is there a tape-recorder available for recording the interaction? If so, discuss what procedure you should follow to make certain that it is ready for recording at the beginning of your lesson. If not, plan to bring a recorder and discuss where and how it should be located for effective recording.
    c. Discuss the closing procedure. Since you do not know how long the lesson will last, make certain that you know how to return the students at the close of the lab experience. If you will be in another room, determine if it will be appropriate to simply bring the students back to the homeroom when you have completed.
    d. Check to see if a list of students' names is available. If so, make name tags or signboards to take with you. If not, plan to take cards, pins, and a felt-tip pen with you. When you first meet the students, spend several minutes getting acquainted and make name tags or signboards at that time. (Primary students do not mind name tags, but upper grade, junior high, and high school students do. Signboards are acceptable by all age levels.)

5. Conducting the lesson.
    a. Arrive a few minutes in advance of the scheduled time.
    b. Have all materials ready and organized.
    c. When you meet the students for the first time, spend a few minutes getting acquainted. (1) Introduce yourself and tell them something about yourself: who you are and what you are doing there. (2) Find out who they are: their names, what they like about school, what they do for fun, and so on.
    d. Check the tape recorder to see that it is operating correctly. Let the students know that you are required to tape-record and analyze the discussion. Let each give her or his name and address and play it back to check on volume and tone.
    e. When teaching the lesson, *enjoy yourself.* The students are going to enjoy you since you are a break from the usual routine. Don't stick to

the lesson plan so tightly that you lose touch with them. Consider your plan to be a "general road map," to return to in order to reach your destination, and let them take you down a few side roads. Respond naturally, don't try to be a "buddy," don't try to be "the authority"—*be yourself*.

Directions for Taping a Lesson

1. Determine in advance of each teaching experience what recorder you will be using. Practice with this recorder until you are thoroughly familiar with its operation to ensure its effective use. (A relatively high-quality cassette recorder is unquestionably the easiest to operate, and generally produces a high-quality recording.)

2. If possible, use a small group of students (six to twelve). Seat them in a circle or semicircle so that all are approximately the same distance from the microphone (see Chart 3-2).

3. Make certain that the mike is placed on some sort of padded material (eraser, sponge, mitten, etc.) and that it is not immediately next to the recorder. A sensitive mike placed on the same table as the recorder will pick up recorder noise even though you can't hear it.

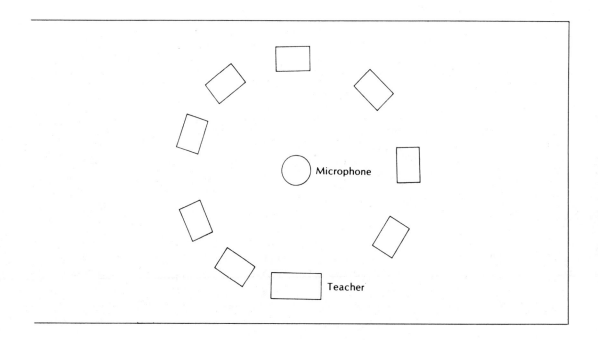

Arrangements for Laboratory Experience

After making the necessary verbal arrangements with the teacher, it will be helpful to send the following letter to clarify the situation.

I would like to express my appreciation for your willingness to provide an opportunity for me to gain understanding and skill in the inquiry teaching process. I know that this places an additional demand on your already busy schedule, and your willingness to assist me is very much appreciated.

In establishing the conditions for this experience, it would be most helpful if the following arrangements could be made:

1. *I would like to work with six to twelve children, not necessarily the most verbal students but students who are likely to participate actively in a discussion. (If possible, I would like to avoid working with children with behavior problems.)*

2. *It would be ideal if the students could be taken to a room separate from your classroom, and brought back when the laboratory experience is over.*

3. *Since it is difficult to know precisely how long the teaching episode will last, specific arrangements will need to be made for returning the children to you at the close of the lesson.*

It is my responsibility to be at your classroom at the precise time that we mutually agree on, and to follow whatever procedures you feel are necessary for working within your school and with your students. If there is anything that I might do to facilitate a successful and enjoyable experience for you and your students, do not hesitate to let me know.

ACTIVITIES: ANALYSIS OF LABORATORY EXPERIENCE

Directions

As soon as possible after completing your teaching experience:

1. Refer to the accompanying "Data Collection Guide" (page 71).

2. Listen to your tape-recording and transcribe the interaction as follows:
   a. In the questions column, list the questions exactly as you asked them. (Not as you intended to ask them, but exactly as you *did* ask them.)
   b. In the intent column, code each *question* according to the action that you intended that question to illustrate: D—describing, E—explaining, P—predicting, and C—choosing.
   c. In the response column, list the first (and possibly the second) student response to each question, exactly as given.
   d. In the effect column, code each *response* according to the language

action it illustrated. (Not the language action you *hoped* the question would elicit, but the language action explicitly evident in the student's response.)

3. Analyze each question and response to see if the effect matches the intent. If not, determine the reason. It's not at all uncommon to design a question to fit a particular style, and yet use words that change it to a different style. Also, one may elaborate on the first question by asking another question, often in a different style, and students may respond to the second, and not the first, intended question.

4. Analyze the data for judgmental statements. Were you able to accept students' explanations without judging them right or wrong, good or bad? There's a big difference between putting yourself in the authority position of judging ideas as "very good," "good idea," or "you're right," and giving supportive statements to encourage thinking such as, "That's an interesting idea," "Take your time, I can see you are giving it careful thought." The difference is in the student responses. Look for it. Are you causing them to be dependent on you for approval or are you facilitating their thinking for themselves? Considerable emphasis will be placed on the importance of this in the next chapter.

Source Notes

1. Benjamin S. Bloom, ed., *Taxonomy of Educational Objectives, Handbook I: Cognitive Domain* (New York: Longmans, Green, 1961), pp. 201–207.
2. Norris M. Sanders, *Classroom Questions: What Kinds?* (New York: Harper & Row, 1966).
3. J. P. Guilford, *The Nature of Human Intelligence* (New York: McGraw-Hill, 1967), p. 63.
4. See, for example, James J. Gallagher, "Classroom Interaction Study" (Urbana: University of Illinois, 1966); Meridith D. Gall, Barbara Dunning, and Rita Weatherby, *Minicourse 9. Higher Cognitive Questioning* (Toronto: Farwest Laboratory for Educational Research and Development, Macmillan Educational Services, 1971); John A. McCollum and Rose Marie Davis, *The Development of Higher Level Thinking Abilities* (Portland, Oreg.: Northwest Regional Educational Laboratory, 1970); and Jack R. Frankel, *Helping Students Think and Value* (Englewood Cliffs, N.J.: Prentice-Hall, 1973), Chap. 5.
5. John A. McCollum and Rose Marie Davis, *The Development of Higher Level Thinking Abilities* (Portland, Oreg.: Northwest Regional Educational Laboratory, 1970).
6. Fred E. Newton, *Facilitating Inquiry in the Classroom* (Portland, Oreg.: Northwest Regional Educational Laboratory, 1970).
7. Susan Miller, *Questioning Strategies* (Portland, Oreg.: Northwest Regional Educational Laboratory, 1971).

Data Collection Guide for Laboratory Experience

Name _____ Date_____

School _____Cooperating Teacher _____Grade Level_____

Content Focus (describe briefly) _____

Intent	Question	Response	Effect

4 *Interpreting*

Overview

Rationale

The process of inquiry is the set of intellectual operations by which an individual generates personal meanings of what is "right," or "good," or "true." It is a process by which an individual, when confronted with a problem or issue, seeks information, analyzes relationships, and generates personal ideas of why things happen as they do. In other words, it is the process of generating personal meaning as opposed to being told "*the* meaning" by someone else.

The process can be easily seen in the intellectual activity of reading. A good writer does not explicitly state the main idea of the story and then proceed to support it. On the contrary, incidents are presented that allow readers to perceive relationships and generalize for themselves. A skilled writer may very well present the incidents in a manner that leads systematically toward one conclusion but, in the final analysis, the "meaning" of the story is generated by the reader, never by the writer.

General Objectives

At the conclusion of this chapter, you will have developed:

- An understanding of the phrase *interpreting process* and the relationship of that term to the term *inquiry* and other terms that researchers and curriculum developers have given to cognitive processes identified as basic to generating and testing knowledge.

- An understanding of the conditions that facilitate the effective implementation of the interpreting (inquiry) process.

- The ability to discriminate, classify, and design "open" and "closed" questions.

- The ability to design describing, explaining, predicting, and choosing questions and to sequence them into logical order for interpreting story content.

- The ability to conduct a classroom discussion in which the interpreting process is implemented according to prescribed criteria.

Theory and Strategy

To understand the methodology of inquiry, you should be familiar with the differences between two commonly advocated approaches to teaching—the *deductive* and the *inductive* approaches.

Deductive Process

The deductive process is basically one of supplying the generalization or explanation and then supplying specific information to support it.

Methodology (Teaching or Writing Process)

1. Present the generalization or explanation: "Strikes are often caused by social and economic unrest." "Friction occurs when any two substances rub together." "When hurt, people often react in a highly aggressive manner."

2. Present the specific information (data) that support the generalization or explanation.

3. Present problems and events that verify the usefulness of the generalization or explanation.

In this process, an authority (the teacher or textbook) outside of the learner is normally responsible for presenting both the generalization and the proof. The learner's role is one of passive acceptance. Much of the content taught in school is presented through this approach. Most textbooks present rules, definitions, and generalizations and follow them with data to illustrate their validity. This is an effective and expedient way of transmitting certain basic information. However, it deletes the "meaning making" process by which ideas are generated, and it implies that there are always certain "right answers" and "absolute truths." This implication, of course, is simply not accurate, but even if it were, the ultimate goal of the teacher is not merely to distribute answers and truths but to nurture and cultivate minds skilled in the complex information processing that can move toward meaning and toward resolution of the myriad conflicts of life. With this in mind, whenever we find it useful or necessary to employ the deductive process, we must guard against the usual implication that this fact, this principle, this idea is "true" because it comes to us from the unchallengeable heights of authority.

Inductive Process

In the inductive process, learning is basically a procedure of *confronting* a specific event, problem, or issue; *acquiring* and *describing* a body of information related to the event, problem, or issue; *analyzing* causal relationships; and stating *explanations* that are logically supported by the data. The teacher never states the generalization. The students are asked to arrive at such statements from the basis of known data.

Methodology (Teaching or Writing Process)

1. Present an event, problem, or issue to be confronted and explained.

2. Facilitate the acquisition of specific data relative to the problem or issue.

3. Facilitate the analysis of relationships within the data and the statement of generalizations or explanations based on the data: "Strikes are often caused by social and economic unrest." "Friction occurs when any two substances rub together." "When hurt, people often react in a highly aggressive manner."

Synonymous Terms

The scientific enterprise of generating knowledge is accomplished through the inductive process of confronting problems, acquiring data, developing explanations based on the data, and subsequently testing them by either making and checking predictions based on their application to a new situation or by observing how usefully they account for alternative related situations. In this sense (and in this program), the phrases *inquiry process, interpreting process, discovery process,* and *inductive knowledge-generating and testing process* are synonymous and interchangeable. Also, the labels given to the "product" of this process are synonymous and interchangeable. That is, the terms *generalization, explanation, theory, inference,* and *hypothesis* are considered to be the same—each is an "idea," a product of the process whereby an individual confronts an event, problem, or issue, analyzes relationships, and states a probable cause.

The Process of Generating and Testing Knowledge

In the instructional program on inquiry developed by Fred Newton, an illustration is given of a child intuitively engaged in the process of building and testing ideas.

Bill has just finished building a model glider. He is in a local park ready to test-glide it. He gets down on one knee to keep close to the ground for the plane's first test flight. Then quickly, but gently, he pushes the plane forward as he releases it. The nose of the plane rises sharply until it points almost straight up. Suddenly it stops in midair, falls backward, rolls over, and hits the ground almost straight on.

"Must have thrown it up," Bill says to himself. After checking for damage, he repeats his throw, making sure this time that he throws the glider in a straight line. The plane repeats its erratic flight, again hitting the ground nose first.

This time he carefully points the nose down slightly as he releases it. The craft repeats its performance, hitting the ground sharply a third time.

"Now, why does it do that?" Bill murmurs to himself.

"Maybe it has something to do with weight. Maybe the nose of the airplane needs to be heavier." It suddenly strikes him that if he moves the wing to the rear it might be less likely to "nose up" in flight.

"Sure, the wing is what lifts the airplane. The wing is like a balance point. It's doing that because the nose isn't heavy enough. If I move the wing back farther it should fly smoother."

He then shifts the wing a bit to the rear and releases the glider in a straight line as he did before. Now the craft has less tendency to stall. The flight path is more smooth.

By shifting the wing farther and farther to the rear during a carefully sequenced series of trials, Bill finds he can make the glider fly as he wishes, and to make a smooth landing.

"At last," he thinks.[1]

The process Bill engaged in illustrates the scientific knowledge-building process by which ideas are generated and tested. For example, Bill is searching for a way to make his airplane follow a smooth glide path. In his initial trial, the flight path was quite erratic and he generated the *explanation,* "It is caused by the way I throw it," and *predicted,* "If I throw it in a straight line it will fly smoothly." When it stalled again, he rejected his previous explanation on the basis of the new data and came up with another *explanation:* "The wing is like a balance point. It's doing that because the nose isn't heavy enough." From this explanation he formulated a new *prediction:* "If I move the wing back farther so that more weight is forward of the wing, it should fly smoother." Each explanation is *tested* until a test confirms his explanation.

The intellectual process is:

1.   Confronting a problem or event (content focus).

2.   Generating data.

3.   Formulating an explanation based on the data.*

4.   Testing the explanation by predicting.

Thus, when building and testing ideas, three language actions are apparent:

Describing: Data are generated.

Explaining: Explanations are formulated on the basis of the data.

Predicting: Predictions are made, based on the explanations.

The knowledge-generating and testing processes can be diagrammed as:

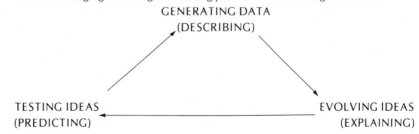

GENERATING DATA
(DESCRIBING)

TESTING IDEAS
(PREDICTING)

EVOLVING IDEAS
(EXPLAINING)

---

*   Other terms commonly used to label this cognitive operation are *inferring, generalizing, hypothesizing,* and *theorizing.*

In the example, Bill generated meaning for himself in a completely natural, autonomous, inquiring manner.* What he arrived at, through a natural process of generating and testing *his* meaning of *his* world, was a solution that *worked*. The *describing, explaining, predicting* process resulted in a solution for the "problem" (or puzzle or discrepancy).

Facilitating Inquiry in the Classroom

There are two ways that teachers can facilitate the inquiry process in the classroom. One is by simply *allowing* it to happen naturally, as Bill solved his glider problem. This means providing opportunities where problem identification and solving can occur in a natural manner. It means planning a learning environment in which students are confronted naturally with phenomena and events that elicit curiosity and inquiry. The environment should be rich in illustrations of real life or simulated applications of the content being studied.

A second way that teachers can facilitate this process in the classroom is to *cause* it to happen. Inquiry can occur at any level and in any curriculum area, but it requires a teacher who has the understanding and skills to prepare and implement a strategy that causes students to generate and test ideas. The strategy involves asking questions rather than relying on the natural, spontaneous process in which the students ask their own questions. For example, suppose a number of plants have been grown under similar conditions. A student, when asked, "Why are some plants almost white while others are various shades of green?" might respond with the explanation, "Plants must have sunlight to grow." Then at least two different testing questions can be asked: "Do you expect the plants covered with aluminum foil to die?" *(predicting)* or: "How would this relate to the claim made by many foresters that cutting trees increases the yield of a forest?" *(explaining)*. Both questions cause the student to consider the usefulness of his or her idea. Thus the interpreting process is one in which students are encouraged to generate their own *personal* meanings. However, it also includes the equally important process of testing the degree to which the idea is useful. But facilitating the process—testing the idea—requires the highest degree of skill on the part of the teacher.

Chart 4-1 presents an outline of the steps in this instructional process.

The first step is *generating descriptions*.† The action called for involves identifying and *describing* specific observations selected from a body of information. The questions call for *describing*:

"How did Sally behave toward her friend?"

"What happened when we added acid?"

"What industries do we find in Bolivia?"

---

*   It has been claimed by some that inquiry requires a "mature, adult" mind. Nonsense! Often the mature adult has lost the ability to inquire.

†   Conducting the first two steps requires that you become sensitive to the appropriateness of either judging or simply accepting the students' comments. This will be discussed in detail in "Acceptance," pages 83–84.

Interpreting Procedure

CHART 4-1

PURPOSE	LANGUAGE ACTION	QUESTIONS
Acquiring and examining specific information.	*Describing* specific observations selected from a body of data.	"How did Sally behave toward her friend?" "What is in the liquid?
Generating explanations (generalizing, theorizing, hypothesizing, or inferring).	*Explaining* cause-effect relationships between sets of observations.	"How do you account for the differences in their behavior?" "Why did the liquid change color?"
Testing explanations.	*Predicting* consequences of applying a previously generated explanation to a new situation, or *explaining* a new situation based on a previously generated idea.	"How might you feel in a similar situation?" "What would be the results of using this liquid to water plants?" "How do you account for some plants being white?"

The second step is *generating explanations*. The action called for involves identifying causal relationships and *explaining* the cause-and-effect relationship between sets of observations. The questions call for *explaining*:

"How do you account for the differences in their behavior?"

"How does the rainfall of Oregon affect its economy?"

"Why did the substance change state?"

The third step is *testing explanations*. The action called for involves either: *predicting* the consequences of applying previously generated explanation(s) to a new situation:

"How might the story have gone if Toshi and Oji-san had been selfish and greedy?"

"Based on our ideas of how plants grow, what would happen if we planted grass seeds instead of beans?"

or *explaining* a new situation based on a previously generated explanation:

"If overproduction causes a reduction in prices, how do you account for rising prices in the automobile industry?"

Applying the Inquiry Process

The application of this process to interpreting a specific story is illustrated in the following:

Material: *The Golden Crane* by Tohr Yamaguchi[2]

Objective: To become aware that people face a conflict of values between altruistic (to give love) and selfish (to obtain things) desires*

Resume of *The Golden Crane,* a Japanese folktale:[2]

Toshi, a deaf and dumb orphan boy, is cared for by Oji-san, a very old, but highly skilled fisherman. Toshi finds a wounded golden crane, a bird considered holy. Together they not only nurse the sacred bird to health but defend it against all others, including the Emperor, who wish to exploit it for their own gain. In the end, Toshi speaks, and both Toshi and Oji-san are rescued from punishment from the Emperor's men and carried on the wings of the golden crane into the rising sun.

Step 1: *Generating descriptions*

"What happened in the story that you thought was interesting?"

"What happened that told you how Toshi and Oji-san felt about the golden crane?"

"What happened that told you how the others in the story felt about the golden crane?"

Step 2: *Generating explanations*

"How do you account for the differences in the way Toshi and Oji-san behaved toward the crane, and the way others behaved toward it?"

"Why do you think Toshi was able to talk and was carried away by the bird?"

"How do you think this story might have a meaning for all people?"

Step 3: *Testing explanations*

a. *Predicting*

"What might happen to the beautiful things in nature around us if we all behaved like the others in the story all the time?"

"Do you think the people in our society who do good will be rewarded for their good deeds?"

b. *Explaining*

"How do you account for most parks having rules that prohibit people picking flowers to take home with them, or that most states do not allow people to catch wild birds and animals for pets?"

---

*   The author of a story (as well as a curriculum developer) builds an experience deductively. That is, the author has a generalization in mind and builds data deductively to support that idea. However, readers progress through the story (data) "inductively" to discover the meaning for themselves—that is, they interpret the idea presented. An "interpreting" question sequence is designed to facilitate this inductive process.

INTERPRETING

The first question is an open question that calls for any observation the students might wish to give. Asking an open question initially provides a base of specific information from which to proceed, and, more importantly, allows every student to become involved without having to "read the teacher's mind."

Once you have this base of information, you can ask closed describing questions that call for specific observations. Here the purpose is to elicit specific evidence that supports the cause-and-effect relationship you will subsequently consider. In this case, descriptions were called for about Toshi and Oji-san's behavior toward the crane, followed by asking for descriptions of how others behaved.

After identifying and describing specific observations, students are asked to generate explanations of the cause-and-effect relationship. In this case, they were first asked, "How do you account for the differences in the way Toshi and Oji-san behaved toward the crane and the way others behaved toward it?" The purpose of this question is to cause students to generate interpretations about the basic conflict the author is presenting. They are guided to focus their thinking on that particular conflict situation. This is followed by, "Why do you think Toshi was able to talk and was carried away by the bird at the end?" and "How do you think this story may have meaning for all people?" These questions are designed to cause students to move beyond the specific data in the story to give their personal interpretations of the symbolic rescue and reward of the injured crane, Toshi, and Oji-san.

After explaining the cause-and-effect relationships, the final step of the interpreting process asks students to consider the usefulness of their explanations by using them to predict future consequences or to account for (explain) a new situation. Obviously, you cannot determine in advance, with absolute accuracy, what the students' responses will be when asked to generate explanations. However, if the *describing* questions have been designed to elicit specific evidence to support a particular cause-and-effect relationship, and the *explaining* questions have focussed directly on that cause-and-effect relationship, you can predict with a considerable degree of accuracy what the responses to the explaining questions are likely to be, and on that basis testing questions can be formulated in advance. In this case, you can expect responses like: "Toshi and Oji-san loved the bird and wanted to help it." "The others were selfish and wanted to possess it for themselves." "Good is rewarded and selfishness is punished." The testing questions were designed to cause students to consider the usefulness of these ideas by using them to predict consequences in their own world of the values they discovered in the story and/or to explain a new situation in their experience in light also of their discoveries from the story and discussion. By tuning in carefully to the responses that students give to the explaining questions, and by responding to the ideas presented in a natural, relaxed, and *interested* manner, you will do much to assist students to test their own ideas.

Illustrations of the Inquiry Process

Following are two additional examples of the process. The first illustrates an interpreting question sequence that might be implemented in the discussion of a newspaper article, the second illustrates the process applied to a science event.

Content Focus:
Material: Weekly news magazine article on Antarctica.
Objective: Animals are uniquely adapted to their environment.

Open Describing Question:

> **"What are some of the things the article told us about Antarctica?"**

Closed Describing Questions:

> **"What is the climate like in Antarctica?"**
>
> **"What grows there?"**
>
> **"What animal life do they have there?"**
>
> **"How are the animals in Antarctica different from those in (Oregon)?"**

Explaining Questions:

> **"How are the animals able to live there?"**

Testing Questions:

> **"What might happen if we took some of our (Oregon) animals to Antarctica?"**
>
> **"How do you account for some animals having thin fur and others having thick fur?"**

In an interpreting process where the content focus is an article, story, film, or information display (where data are explicitly evident), the process is simply:

1. Describing points in the data.

2. Explaining cause-and-effect relationships.

3. Making predictions and/or explanations based on the explanations generated.

The following illustration is from a science instruction, where students are presented with an event from which they must generate their own data, develop explanations based on the data, and make predictions based on the explanations.

Content Focus:
Material: Science experiment.
Objective: Certain conditions must exist for plants to grow.

Introduction (Teacher): "For the next two weeks we will be examining how plants grow. I have here some bean seeds, some containers, some gravel, dirt, and water. I would like each of you to plant a bean seed and take care of it for two weeks. You can use any of these materials and you can put it anywhere you like in the room; however, once you have placed your container in a location, leave it there for the full two weeks.

"Each of you is to describe in a notebook exactly what you do to the plant, from the time you start until the time that we share information. Describe what materials you used and exactly how you planted it. Also, as many times as you wish during the next two weeks, observe the plant and describe what you see. Each time, record the day and the time of the day when you made your observation."

Open Describing Question (Two Weeks Later):

"Now that we have observed our plants for two weeks, let's share what we found out. What did you observe?"

Closed Describing Questions:

"What happened to those plants that were planted in just gravel?"

"What happened to those plants that were placed on the window sill?"

"What happened to those plants that received over two quarts of water?"

Explaining Questions:

"Why did some plants grow taller than others?"

"Why did some plants have a different color?"

"Why did two of the plants die?"

Testing Question:

"Now that we have some explanations about how plants respond to growing conditions, we will again plant some seeds, this time grass seeds. Some we'll place in dirt, some in gravel and dirt mixed, some in just gravel. We will water some with 10 cc of water a day, and some with 2 cc of water a day. Some we will place in the window, some will be placed in the closet. Based on our explanations of how plants grow, what do you predict will happen to these new plants?"

This example illustrates the inductive knowledge-generating and testing process of:

1.   Acquiring and describing data.

2.   Developing explanations.

3.   Making predictions based on the explanations.

Basic Question Strategy

1.   *Open Describing Question*

a. *Objectives:* As a result of asking an open describing question that calls for any observation from the data being interpreted, students will:
   (1) present a universe of ideas that represent their conceptualizations of the event being discussed, and
   (2) all students will be given the opportunity to become initially involved in the discussion without having to produce a specific response.

b. *Illustrative Questions:*

"What did you see in the film?"

"What happened in the story?"

"What things happened that interested you?"

"What did you see take place in the experiment?"

"What have we been able to find out about Bolivia?"

2. *Closed Describing Questions*
   a. *Objective:* As a result of asking a closed describing question (or a series of closed describing questions), students will respond with focussed or selected statements of observations from the field of data.
   b. *Illustrative Questions:*

"What did the film tell us about transportation?"

"What did Toshi do when the Emperor arrived?"

"What happened when we added acid to the solution?"

"What industries do they have in the coastal area?"

3. *Explaining Questions*
   a. *Objective:* As a result of asking an explaining question (or a series of explaining questions), students will respond with appropriate statements of cause-and-effect relationships between sets of observations.
   b. *Illustrative Questions:*

"How do you account for the difference in expressed feelings?"

"How does the climate affect farm products in this country?"

"Why are some of the plants bright green while others are almost white?"

4. *Testing Questions*
   a. *Objective:*
      (1) As a result of asking a predicting question (or series of predicting questions) based on previously generated explanations, students will respond with hypotheses that logically apply the explanations to a new or future situation, or

    (2)   As a result of asking an explaining question (or series of explaining questions), students will respond with statements that utilize a previously generated explanation to account for a new situation.

b.   *Illustrative Questions:*

"To what extent do you think this might be true of all cultures?"

"Based on our bean seed experiments, what do you think will happen to our grass seeds?"

"Then how do you account for the ones covered with aluminum foil being still alive?"

Basic Discussion Skills

Seeking Personal Meaning   The importance of tuning-in on what students are saying cannot be overemphasized. You must keep in mind that students express themselves with two kinds of words—*report words,* which to a greater or lesser degree have commonly agreed-on referents in the real world, depending on the shared experiences of the discussants, and *inferential-judgmental words,* which have meaning only to the individual using the word. You must make every effort to bring about a shared understanding of personal word meanings.

Acceptance   Another especially important part of effectively conducting the inquiry process is developing sensitivity as to when it is and is not appropriate to judge students' comments. It is appropriate at the *describing* level to judge the accuracy of observations. At this point, it is important to have accurate data as a basis for making subsequent generalizations. Thus, at this point, it is perfectly appropriate to say something like, "I don't think that is accurate, is it, Jim? Check it again, please." However, at the *explaining* level (unless specific criteria for acceptable performance are specified in advance), *all* explanations should be accepted without judging them right or wrong, good or bad, strong or weak—and without changing them or editorializing on them.

For teachers who have spent their entire lives in personal, social, and academic systems based on right answers and absolute truths according to arbitrary authority, this teaching behavior of accepting ideas without judging them is probably the most difficult to implement. However, the whole meaning-making, knowledge-generating, and testing process depends on the students acquiring the understanding and skill to evaluate their own ideas. *Explanations have strength to the extent that one can control or predict on the basis of them.* Acquiring the ability to test generated explanations is an integral part of the process. The teacher must not deny students the right to test their own ideas.

Supporting   An essential behavior, which must operate in conjunction with acceptance, is creating an environment of psychological support for the learner. Students need to be made to feel that they are worthy, acceptable individuals and that the ideas they have are worthy and acceptable. This can generally only be fostered in an atmosphere in which the teacher treats students as though he or she honestly *believes* them to be worthy, acceptable, and effective individuals. It's difficult to talk about an environment of support except in generalities; however, it is clearly demonstrated in such teacher responses as:

"Go ahead, express it any way you like."

"Take a minute to think."

"Would you like me to come back to you later?"

Acceptance vs. Supporting   Obviously there is a fine line that distinguishes the differences between accepting a student's idea without judging it and giving the student the psychological support she or he needs in order to feel good about herself or himself. However, the difference is in the effect of the language used by the teacher. For example, note the differences in the following teacher responses, all of which use judgmental language:

"O.K."

"I like that."

"I understand."

"Very good."

The specific effect of each of these expressions can only be determined by actually analyzing what happens in a class when they are used. However, more than likely, you would find the effect to be as follows:

"O.K." A routine, rhetorical expression that is equated with discussion management. "O.K., next." Students learn to ignore it.

"I like that." A report of feelings. The effect could be students continually striving to please the teacher, but if the relationships are really open, honest, and direct, the psychological climate is not likely to be one of dependency.

"I understand." Again, a report of inner state. Generally very effective in supporting independent thinking, particularly if followed with a paraphrase.

"Very good." A statement of authority. The idea is valuable, not because it is useful but because the teacher has judged it as good. An established pattern of use can result in an established pattern of students always seeking approval from the authority.

Again, the line that distinguishes the difference between judging and supporting often seems intangible. However, it generally shows up quite clearly in the interaction of the classroom. Students either depend on the teacher or they depend on themselves for determining what is "true" or "right" or "good." Chart 4-2 illustrates the differences between the two approaches.

Judging vs. Supporting Teaching Approaches

CHART 4-2

INTERACTION	TEACHER AS JUDGE	TEACHER AS FACILITATOR
Setting the Focus	"I want you to read the text and be prepared to tell me the three causes of . . . ."	"Let's get into as many sources as possible to try to find clues as to why this might happen. Our text should be particularly helpful."
Conducting the Discussion	"O.K. Who can tell me what the three causes are."	"What have we been able to find out that might explain why . . . happened?"
Responding to Ideas	"Very good, Susan! Exactly right!"	"That's an interesting idea, Susan. Let's test it to see if it works in other situations."

Open vs. Closed Questions

Within any classroom discussion, teacher questions either facilitate or inhibit verbal interaction. For example, the following two excerpts of classroom discussions illustrate contrasting lessons. The first, Science Lesson 1, will be easily recognized as a discussion characterized by very little pupil response, while the second, Science Lesson 2, is characterized by much pupil response. Pay particular attention to the teacher's questions and the responses they elicit. Also, speculate about the feeling of these two classes. Comfortable? Relaxed? Tense? Bored? Excited?

Science Lesson 1

Students are in their seats with attention focussed on the teacher at the demonstration table. The teacher holds up a bimetallic strip.

Teacher: **"Does anyone know what this is called?"**

Jim: **"It looks like a knife."**

Teacher: **"Well, yes, but it has a special name, does anyone know it?"**

(Short silence)

Teacher: **"It's called a bimetallic strip, and it has some very special properties. Watch closely while I demonstrate."**

The teacher holds the bimetallic strip in a Bunsen burner flame and it bends down. Then the strip is placed in a beaker of clear liquid and it straightens out. The teacher carefully turns the strip over and again holds it in the flame. This time the strip bends up.

Class: Several "Ohs" and "Ahs" and "Hey, look at that!"

Teacher: **"O.K. Can any of you recall what you read in the chapter assigned yesterday? What is this? What's causing this?"**

(Short silence)

Teacher: **"How many of you read that chapter?"**

Class: Most raise their hands.

Teacher: **"All right, what did you find out about heat?"**

Robert: **"Mr. Smith, why did it bend that way?"**

Teacher: **"That's what I'd like you to explain. What did you find out about heat and its effect on metals?"**

(Short silence)

Betty: **"Well, the heat will cause any metal to melt at a certain temperature."**

Teacher: **"Very good. Betty, what's that point called?"**

Betty: **"Melting point?"**

Teacher: **"Right! Now can anyone recall anything else they read in that chapter?"**

Susan: **"Heat makes metal expand."**

Teacher: **"Excellent, Susan, excellent! What would that have to do with the bimetallic strip experiment?"**

(Short silence)

Teacher: **"Well, let me give you a clue. As you might guess from its name, this strip is made of two metals fused together. What difference would that make? What would be the effect of heat being applied to two different metals?"**

Science Lesson 2

Pupils have been assigned to worktables supplied with bowls of ice, running water, gas burners, and bimetallic strips fitted into wooden handles.

Teacher: **"All right, class, you remember that in the unit on weather we just finished, one of the things we studied was the effect, or I should say the effects, of temperature on the behavior of air masses. To-day we'll begin to take a look at heat in relation to the behavior of** matter. I am purposely not going to say much more about it for now. You will find a variety of materials at the tables. With the understanding that we are concerned with heat and matter, see if you can discover relationships or puzzles that you can report back to the class in about thirty minutes. O.K., go ahead. Distribute yourselves about three to a table. I'll walk about the lab as you're working."

(The pupils disperse and in thirty minutes are asked to reassemble for discussion)

Teacher: "O.K., what's been happening?"

Robert: "What I'd like to know is what kind of crazy thing is this?"

(Holds up a bimetallic strip)

Tony: "Yeah, it just ain't human!"

Teacher: "Something about it puzzles you?"

Berny: "Yeah, what makes it bend like that?"

Susan: "It doesn't make sense. No matter which side you put the flame on, it always bends in the same direction. And when you cool it, it goes the other way."

Robert: "And why should it bend anyhow? If you put a knife into a flame, it doesn't bend."

Sonya: "Maybe if the knife was thin enough . . ."

Robert: "Now, even a spatula, which I thought this thing was, I never saw one do that."

Mildred: "Have you tried it?"

Arnie: "Mr. Glass, is this a spatula?"

Teacher: "I suppose you could use it for that, but no, as a matter of fact, it's a piece of laboratory equipment used for certain kinds of demonstrations."

Lenny: "Another thing, it doesn't stay bent. If you just let it cool to room temperature, it goes back to straight, to the way it was."

Robert: "I don't get it."

Teacher: "Well, look, do you remember how I introduced you to this material?"

Sonya: "You told us that we were going to study about heat and matter."

Teacher: "That's right. Anything else? Can anybody remember anything that might be relevant to this thing that's confusing you?"

(Silence)

Teacher: "O.K., what do you remember about heat and air?"

Lenny: "Warm air rises."

Teacher: "Why?"

Lenny: "Because it expands."

Teacher: "Uh huh. What makes it do that?"

Mildred: "Oh yeah, I remember. Heat is a form of energy, it makes the molecules of air dance, sort of, it makes them bounce against each other harder or faster."

Robert: "So that for a certain number of molecules, they take up more space because they need more room. Also, when they take up more room, the air weighs less so it rises."

Andrew: "So what's that got to do with this stuff?"

Sonya: "Maybe the heat makes the metal expand and that's why it bends."

(Animated cross conversation and argument)

Andrew: "That's stupid! If it expanded, it would just get bigger, it wouldn't bend! Anyhow, metal's not like air, it can't float around the same way. It doesn't have molecules."

Frances: "I thought everything is made of atoms or molecules?"

(Silence)

Lenny: "Is that right, Mr. Glass?"

Teacher: "Well, why don't we assume that it is and then see what effects that assumption has on your conclusions?"

Discussion Focus Setting

At this point, let's examine in greater detail the characteristics of the questions utilized by these two teachers. The question that initiates a discussion has much to do with the level and extent of subsequent verbal interaction. Recall the initial questions of the two teachers:

Teacher 1: "Does anyone know what this is called?"

Teacher 2: "O.K. What's been happening?"

Undoubtedly you recognized that teacher 1 began the discussion with a very narrow, closed question. That is not the only reason for the lack of student involvement in the discussion, but it certainly contributed. Such a question can only be answered by one word or phrase, only one student can normally respond, and there is only one right answer. The rest of the class is closed off from contributing. Teacher 2, on the other hand, initiated the discussion with a wide-open question. Not only could every student in the class respond, but every student could respond comfortably and successfully.

We can generalize (explain) that initiating a discussion with an open question results in more pupil involvement and an interpresonal climate that is more open, relaxed, and comfortable.

Patterns of Questions

Closed Question: Calls for one word or short, predictable answer. Usually calls for remembered factual data.*

Multiple Questions: Two or more questions asked together in a sequence, the last often changing the focus of the first. Because this change of focus often results in confusion, this type of teacher question has the effect of inhibiting discussion.

Open Question: Calls for extended response. Calls for pupil-initiated ideas. Often calls for thinking beyond the memory level.

EXERCISES: PATTERNS OF QUESTIONS

Directions

The following is a series of questions taken from a third-grade social studies discussion. Examine each question and classify it as:

OQ—Open question

CQ—Closed question

MQ—Multiple question

_____ 1. "Yesterday we visited the Health Department of our city. What are some of the things the workers do who work at this department?"

_____ 2. "What is the head of the Health Department called?"

_____ 3. "Why and how do they plan for the city streets and so forth in this office?"

_____ 4. "What did the Health Department do with the spoiled bread?"

_____ 5. "What else, besides looking at the food, might health inspectors do in a restaurant?"

---

*   Closed questions can be valuable elicitors of observations, so don't conclude that you should always avoid them.

Answers and Explanations

<u>OQ</u> 1. This is definitely an open question used as a discussion focus. Any child in the class should feel free and comfortable about responding to this question.

<u>CQ</u> 2. This question is closed because it asks for one specific, predictable, factual answer. This is not to say that it is not an important or worthwhile question to ask, but to note that it does not elicit extended, pupil-initiated ideas.

<u>MQ</u> 3. Although this question was probably intended to be open, it is actually a multiple question. The pupils were really asked to respond to two questions: "Why do they plan . . . ?" and "How do they plan . . . ?" Also, the phrase "and so forth" is extremely ambiguous. Place yourself in a pupil's role and imagine how difficult it would be to respond to this question.

<u>CQ</u> 4. This is classified as closed because any logical answer would be specific and predictable. Again, it should not be inferred that this is not a good question to ask.

<u>OQ</u> 5. This is an open question because it does not necessarily call for specific, predictable, remembered responses. The phrase "what might they do?" allows for freedom of response.

Directions

Again, identify teacher questions as open (OQ), closed (CQ), or multiple (MQ). These questions are from a seventh-grade discussion.

_____ 1. "What's your evaluation of how well you have learned in this class?"

_____ 2. "What are you able to do now that you couldn't do before, or, what's the most important thing you've learned?"

_____ 3. "Jim, does coming up with good answers make you feel powerful?"

_____ 4. "In what ways can you tell how well you are doing?"

_____ 5. "What's the meaning of an A grade?"

Answers and Explanations

<u>OQ</u> 1. If this is asked as the beginning question of a class discussion, it should elicit multiple responses and any student should be able to respond successfully.

<u>MQ</u> 2. These are two distinctly different questions calling for two distinctly different responses.

<u>CQ</u> 3. This requests a one-word response from one student.

<u>OQ</u> 4. This will elicit multiple responses from several students.

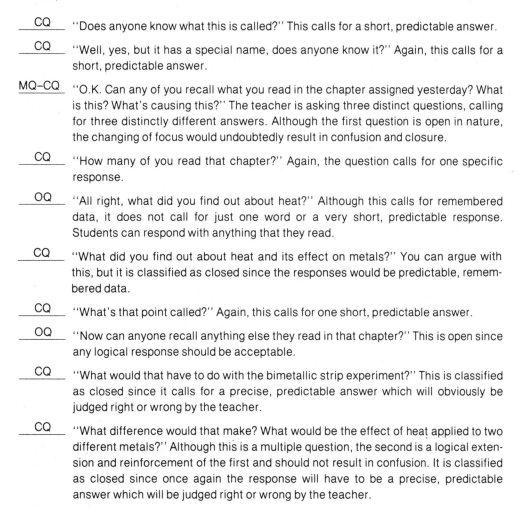

CQ or OQ 5. This is one of those questions that requires your being there to code effectively. If it was asked as "What is *the* meaning of an A grade?," implying there is only *one* right meaning, it would have to be coded as closed. However, if it was asked in a manner that implied there might be multiple meanings, it would be coded as open. Hopefully, it was asked as the latter.

Now go back to Science Lessons 1 and 2 and classify each of the questions asked by the teachers. When finished, check your answers.

Answers and Explanations for Science Lesson 1

_____CQ_____ "Does anyone know what this is called?" This calls for a short, predictable answer.

_____CQ_____ "Well, yes, but it has a special name, does anyone know it?" Again, this calls for a short, predictable answer.

_____MQ–CQ_____ "O.K. Can any of you recall what you read in the chapter assigned yesterday? What is this? What's causing this?" The teacher is asking three distinct questions, calling for three distinctly different answers. Although the first question is open in nature, the changing of focus would undoubtedly result in confusion and closure.

_____CQ_____ "How many of you read that chapter?" Again, the question calls for one specific response.

_____OQ_____ "All right, what did you find out about heat?" Although this calls for remembered data, it does not call for just one word or a very short, predictable response. Students can respond with anything that they read.

_____CQ_____ "What did you find out about heat and its effect on metals?" You can argue with this, but it is classified as closed since the responses would be predictable, remembered data.

_____CQ_____ "What's that point called?" Again, this calls for one short, predictable answer.

_____OQ_____ "Now can anyone recall anything else they read in that chapter?" This is open since any logical response should be acceptable.

_____CQ_____ "What would that have to do with the bimetallic strip experiment?" This is classified as closed since it calls for a precise, predictable answer which will obviously be judged right or wrong by the teacher.

_____CQ_____ "What difference would that make? What would be the effect of heat applied to two different metals?" Although this is a multiple question, the second is a logical extension and reinforcement of the first and should not result in confusion. It is classified as closed since once again the response will have to be a precise, predictable answer which will be judged right or wrong by the teacher.

The general nature of this discussion might be described as a type of guessing game, with the teacher having precise, predictable answers in mind which she or he searches for with basically closed questions. Typically, the teacher judges and dramatically rewards the correct student response. As a result, the discussion is characterized by teacher–pupil–teacher–pupil interaction, with little evidence of thinking beyond the memory level. We can speculate that the emotional climate of the class probably started with interest and excitement, but ended with boredom or tension.

Answers and Explanations for Science Lesson 2

___OQ___ "O.K. What's been happening?" Obviously this is an open question and will elicit many responses.

___OQ___ "Something about it puzzles you?" The question wasn't "Does it puzzle you?" which would call for a one-word response. The word *something* is an invitation to say what is puzzling, while leaving the possibilities of response open.

___CQ___ "Do you remember how I introduced you to this material?" This calls for a particular answer. However, it is stated in a way that would probably result in more extended responses.

___OQ___ "Can anybody remember anything that might be relevant to this thing that's confusing you?" Again, the pupils are free within fairly wide limits to give any response. One specific, predictable answer is not implied.

___OQ___ "O.K. What do you remember about heat and air?" The question implies that any remembered information will be acceptable.

___OQ___ "Why?" You might dispute this classification; but just the word *why* leaves the response much more open than if the teacher had said, "What are the factors that cause warm air to rise?" That question would be classified as closed since it calls for a specific, predictable response.

___CQ___ "What makes it do that?" This is quite closed. It does call for a specific, predictable answer.

___OQ___ "Well, why don't we assume that it is and then see what effects that assumption has on your conclusions?" This is a direction given in the form of a choice while giving structure to a procedure for moving on.

The general nature of this discussion is certainly one of openness. The questions used by this teacher almost always elicit extended pupil-initiated ideas. As a result, there is much more pupil talk than teacher talk. We might speculate that the emotional climate of this class is characterized by interest and excitement.

ACTIVITIES: OPEN AND CLOSED QUESTIONS

NEW ROCHELLE, N.Y. — When the red light turns to green and reads "Thank You" at any one of the automatic toll booths of the New England Thruway here, it does not always mean what it says. At least not if the motorist has short-changed the machine or dropped lead washers or foreign coins into it.

The state police reported today after a two-week campaign against toll cheaters that they had arrested 151 persons. They have been fined in city court from $25 each for first offenders to $250 for multiple offenders.

Lieutenant Thomas F. Darby reported that the offenders included a clergyman, a doctor, a dentist, an atomic scientist, lawyers, and quite a number of engineers, advertising men, and salesmen.

What the offenders did not know, the lieutenant said, was that new toll-booth glass with one-way vision prevented them from seeing watchful troopers inside. Neither did they know, the lieutenant continued, that the license plate of each offender was recorded, along with the objects he dropped into the machine.[3]

Directions

Consider the above news report as content for a class discussion. Write two open questions and two closed questions that might be asked about it. Be prepared to share your questions with other members of the class.

ACTIVITIES: ANALYSIS OF DISCUSSIONS

This exercise presents two classroom discussions, both intended to be interpreting discussions. However, there are marked differences in the patterns of interaction. Describing and accounting for these differences will help your understanding of the inquiry process.

Both of the following discussions had as their purpose the interpretation of the meaning of *The Golden Crane*.[4] The same teacher conducted both discussions. The two groups of students were in adjoining classrooms in the same school, and represented very similar ability, achievement, and socioeconomic backgrounds.[5]

Directions

Read both discussions and then respond to the directions at the conclusion of discussion 2.

Discussion 1: *The Golden Crane*

Teacher: "What was the meaning of the story *The Golden Crane* to you? Rachel?"

Rachel:	"Well, I can't seem to think."
Teacher:	"Fred?"
Fred:	"Well, it has a lot of golden cranes."
Teacher:	"Golden cranes. What meaning did it have for some of the rest of you? Marian?"
Marian:	"The expression of the words it used."
Teacher:	"Anything else that the story meant to you? Susan, you had some ideas just a little while ago. What did you think that story meant?"
(No answer)
Teacher:	"Sven?"
Sven:	"Well, just about the cranes. No, not just about the cranes but about a Chinese boy and the golden cranes."
Bryan:	"Japanese."
Sven:	"The Japanese boy and the golden cranes."
Teacher:	"Bryan thought it was a Japanese boy. Rachel, did you remember now?"
Rachel:	"Yes. That you shouldn't take things that aren't yours."
Teacher:	"Why do you say that, Rachel? Would you like to explain to us why you thought it meant that?"
Rachel:	"Well, all the other men, they wanted the crane but it wasn't theirs."
Teacher:	"Susan?"
Susan:	"Well, at the end, what the story meant to me was Toshi and the old man, well, they helped the cranes so the cranes helped them by taking them away."
Teacher:	"Fred, you had some ideas?"
Fred:	"Well, see, like the fisherman, well, he just helped the bird to get well, and the Emperor wanted the bird and the fisherman said that he was going to get it, that's all."
Teacher:	"Fred?"
Fred:	"When the golden birds came, they took the man and the boy, and then the boy could talk."
Edwin:	"And he could hear, too."
Teacher:	"Edwin, what was that?"
Edwin:	"He could hear, too."
Teacher:	"Sue Anne?"
Sue Anne:	"Well, in almost every story, there's a theory, and in this story there's a theory, too. Not to order things that are not yours."
Teacher:	"So you felt the story had a lesson to teach us. Any other ideas about the meaning of the story? Rachel?"
Rachel:	"Well, just that you should try to help other people and other things."
Brad:	"You shouldn't order people to give you things that aren't yours."
Teacher:	"Any other ideas? Sherrill, did you have any ideas? Did you enjoy the story?"

Students:	"Yessss!"
Teacher:	"Why did you like the story?"
Students:	"Because it was good."

Discussion 2: *The Golden Crane*

Teacher:	"What happened that told you how Toshi felt about the golden bird? Jim?"
Jim:	"Well, you could tell how he felt, that he liked the golden bird because he didn't want anyone to take him because they belonged to, he belonged to, he should be free, and he didn't belong in a cage, and stuff like this."
Teacher:	"Any other ideas, Nancy?"
Nancy:	"In the story he adored them."
Teacher:	"Anything else in the story that told you how Toshi felt about the golden bird? Robbie?"
Robbie:	"Well, this may be what Nancy said that right at the end, he stood up and he put his arms up and he said to the birds that he adored them."
Teacher:	"Cliff?"
Cliff:	"He didn't want the crane to be caged up."
Teacher:	"Don, what were you going to say?"
Don:	"The same thing."
Teacher:	"What happened in the story that told you how the other people felt about the bird? Gregg?"
Gregg:	"Well, the golden crane was a holy bird so that they wanted to see it because they had never seen one close up."
Teacher:	"Sally?"
Sally:	"They wanted to buy it because they thought it was so golden."
Teacher:	"Blake?"
Blake:	"Well, they wanted to buy it because they thought it was so valuable, because the feathers were pure gold, and, well, they wanted to steal feathers and everything, and they wanted to get closer so they could do that and stuff."
Teacher:	"Jackie?"
Jackie:	"Well, they called Toshi and what's-his-name a fool because they didn't want to sell the bird."
Teacher:	"Did you have something, Jim? You had your hand raised."
Jim:	"He said it."
Teacher:	"Don?"
Don:	"Well, they thought the bird was from heaven, well, they kinda, you know, they thought it was a big thing."
Teacher:	"Nancy, you had something to contribute."
Nancy:	"Well, they thought it was oh, a holy bird sent from heaven and that it was a miracle that one was there."

Teacher:	"Why do you suppose that the villagers' feelings were different from those of Oji-san and Toshi? Why didn't they feel the same way towards the bird? Don, any idea?"
Don:	"Well, they thought the bird would be good because of its riches and they thought it would be like a prince or something to have the only golden bird that there was. Well, not the only one, but the only one that was found."
Teacher:	"Peggy?"
Peggy:	"Well, like she said, they thought that it would be real great. Everyone would think they were real great and come flocking to their house, so they'd get to charge rent and all the people would come to their house just to see this bird and they thought it was a big thing to have it caged because no bird like that had ever been caged."
Teacher:	"Why do you suppose that they felt differently than Toshi and Oji-san did?"
Stan:	"Well, for one thing they didn't have it at their place and they were a little bit jealous probably."
Teacher:	"So you think jealousy may have been one of the reasons why they felt differently than Oji-san and Toshi did. Give us some other ideas. Sally, you have one?"
Sally:	"Well, Toshi, they knew the bird didn't belong to them. That's why they wouldn't sell it. The village people thought they just wanted all the money."
Teacher:	"Wendy?"
Wendy:	"Well, Toshi and Oji-san, they were a lot closer to the bird because, well, they took him home and they mended his wing, so the bird was like, with them, so they'd be closer to the bird than the villagers."
Mary:	"The people were thinking about the money that they could get. But they were thinking of the bird so they could fly back with it."
Teacher:	"Now let's backtrack a little with you. You used 'they' both times and I'm not sure who you meant."
Mary:	"The people were thinking of the riches, and Toshi and Oji-san were thinking about the bird so that he could be back with his relatives."
Teacher:	"Jim?"
Jim:	"Well, all the people around were sort of selfish because they thought that everyone would be going around paying them money and they thought they'd get lots of money for the golden bird, and you'd give a present to the Emperor and he'd do something real nice. He'd give you a nice position. They were just kind of selfish."
Teacher:	"Nancy?"
Nancy:	"Lots of people didn't realize that it was a free bird and shouldn't be caged up. The old fisherman and the little boy did."
Teacher:	"Don?"
Don:	"Well, to Oji-san and Toshi, the bird was like a pet to them at first. Well,

they didn't want to give it away and they wanted the bird to go back to his brothers and sisters.''

Teacher: ''Robbie, what were you going to say?''

Robbie: ''Well, Oji-san and Toshi didn't want that. I was just thinking that any free animal shouldn't be caged. Like them golden cranes. None of them should be caged.''

Teacher: ''And are you saying that Toshi and Oji-san felt as you do?''

Robbie: ''Yah, and that they might feel kind of awkward if they just let the bird go and be caged up. How would you like to be caged up just like an animal?''

Teacher: ''Hinkie?''

Hinkie: ''Well, it gives me the kind of feeling that people seem to think they are rather superior, 'cause, well, it's all right if they kill an animal and then send it to market and have somebody buy it and cook it and eat it; cannibals are dreadful and, well, they think it's perfectly all right to catch an animal and cage him.''

Teacher: ''Do you think this story has a meaning to it? Was it just a good story or was there some meaning to that story? Leslie?''

Leslie: ''Well, it means that the wild animals should be free and then they can live better. They shouldn't be caged.''

Teacher: ''Blake?''

Blake: ''It really does a good job of showing a man's greed because when they all wanted that bird, the rich man, the, the Lord Governor and the Emperor and all of them, well, they were all greedy and they were willing to pay so much for this bird and it just does a wonderful job of showing that.''

Teacher: ''Jim?''

Jim: ''Well, every story has a meaning, but I think that it shows how greedy we can be sometimes and how the lot nicer people really come out good in the end because they got to go up with the cranes, and the Emperor didn't get mad at them or chop off their heads or anything because they went with the cranes and they were never seen again.''

Teacher: ''Gregg, I think you had your hand up.''

Gregg: ''Well, I think that it has a meaning because if somebody is deaf and dumb and at the end it said that he said, 'Beautiful birds, I adore you,' or something, because that would be a miracle.''

Robbie: ''Well, they must have been from the heavens or how could he have said that?''

Teacher: ''So, Robbie, what are you really saying about the meaning of the story?''

Robbie: ''I'm saying, ah, well, like they said at the beginning of the story, these birds must be holy birds.''

Nancy: ''Well, I think it does a good job of showing how many people don't realize about quite a few things.''

Teacher:	"Can you be more specific? What don't they realize, Nancy?"
Nancy:	"Oh, things like animals. They don't realize that they live, too. They have families just like we do."
Teacher:	"Anything else you had in mind?"
	(No answer)
Teacher:	"Don?"
Don:	"They don't realize the freedom of the birds and how, well, like if they were a bird or if they were wounded, they wouldn't like to be caged up and away from their heavens and stuff. They'd rather have their own freedom."
Teacher:	"Jack?"
Jack:	"Well, birds should be free like us. Well, we're caging other birds up, but what if it were the other way around and the birds came swooping down and grabbed up someone and dumped them in a cage?"
Teacher:	"Do you think this is some of the meaning the author was trying to show in this story?"
Jack:	"Well, that we should let other animals be free."
Teacher:	"Do you have another thought, Nancy?"
Nancy:	"Yah. Now I know what I was going to say. They don't care about other living things except themselves."

Directions

Analyze each discussion to determine your response to the following:

1. What differences do you perceive in the patterns of interaction between these two class discussions?

2. How do you account for the differences between these two discussions?

Be prepared to share your responses with other members of the class.

ACTIVITIES: SELECTING A QUESTION SEQUENCE

Directions

Your purpose for using *The Golden Crane* is to assist your students to develop some degree of personal identification with the conflict between wanting to do a good thing and wanting to obtain or own something. Read the question sequences below and write your reaction to each as a sequence for interpreting the story for this purpose. Feel free, if you are dissatisfied with the questions presented, to design your own set of questions as sequence 5.

Be prepared to share your reactions with the other members of your group at the next class session.

INTERPRETING

Sequence	Reaction
1. "What happened in the story?"	
"What does the story tell you about Toshi?"	
"What could you say you have learned from this story?"	
2. "Why was Toshi happy at the end of the story?"	
"What were your feelings about Toshi?"	
"Why were Toshi and Oji-san friends?"	
"Why do you think the story ended as it did?"	
3. "What happened in the story?"	
"What happened in the story that told you how Toshi felt about the bird?"	
"Why do you think he felt so strongly?"	
"Why do you think others felt differently toward the bird?"	
"How do you think you might feel?"	
4. "Whom did you meet in the story?"	
"What happened to them?"	
"Why did this happen?"	
"How did Toshi feel about Oji-san?"	
"Why do you think he felt that way?"	
"How did Oji-san feel about Toshi?	
"Why do you think he felt that way?"	
"What might you say about people anywhere?"	

5.

ACTIVITIES: DESIGNING A QUESTION SEQUENCE

Directions

The following story, ''It's a Tough World,'' shows a twelve-year-old boy coping with a challenge faced by nearly all children, the challenge of beginning to move from the viewpoint and values of childhood to responsible adulthood. The youngster in the story at first feels that he is only a victim in a tough world, but he begins to find his place in that world when he discovers that he can be himself through responsible action.

Your purpose in using this story is to help your students recognize the significant relatedness of the boy's experience to their own, and to see how self-concept—a sense of self-worth—depends on accepting the challenge to act responsibly in the world. Read the story and design a set of questions to use in interpreting the story for this purpose. Be prepared to share them with other class members.

It's A Tough World[6]

The lousy week was over at last! I thumbed my nose at the school bus as it turned the corner in the rain. Then I stepped into the kitchen — right onto sticky, wet wax. Too late, I remembered the kitchen rugs piled outside on the steps. That was Mom's signal to us kids that the floor was being waxed and to go around to the front door. Mom caught me. "You didn't see the rugs?" she asked in her cold, haughty tone which means she's trying to keep her temper. "Go around to the front, Jonathan!"

I went, but when I came in Mom was fuming. I'd thought I was done getting flak from grownups now that the school week was over — and now this! I made a big thing of kicking off my boots in the entryway, tugging at the zippers, and for good measure I tossed my schoolbooks on the floor. I knew that would get to her.

"All right, Mister!" Mom said in clipped, hard tones. "Carry those boots to the bootbox! Take those books downstairs to your room, and while you're there, start cleaning it."

"You're always picking on me because I'm the oldest!" I said. "You're just mad because I stepped on your waxed floor!" I picked up my boots and books and started

downstairs. "It's my room!" I yelled up to her. "You don't live in it! I do! If I want it messy, it's my business!"

Mom didn't answer me. I knew she was still struggling with her temper. I grumbled, "You're home all day long. Why can't you wax floors in the morning, so they're dry after school?"

That did it. Mom raced down the basement stairs. She can really move when she's mad. She came into my room and stood there with her hands on her hips. Her face had a hard look and she spoke each word like a bullet. "You listen, Jonathan Carey! I don't know what your current problem is! But you're acting mighty like two instead of twelve! You pick a fight, you'll get a fight! You'll clean your room because your mess is no longer just your business! I came in here today with a pile of clothes for you to put away, and found last week's clean wash sitting on the floor in that corner. You'd never bothered to put the clothes away."

Mom went on, "I counted two screwdrivers, one pair of pliers, and a pair of goggles—all of them belong in your dad's workshop. I don't wash clothes so you can wipe the floor with them! When your father lets you use his tools you accept the responsibility for putting them away!"

She paused for breath, not taking her eyes off me, just staring, then she finished, "You'll have the right to criticize the way I organize my days when you spend a full day doing all I do. For now, you'll do exactly as you're told. If you don't like it, just remember it's a tough world, kid!" Then she turned and marched back upstairs.

Tough world! Yeah, but how would a grownup know? They can stand there and talk hard and people have to listen. It's not like being a kid and having to take all the hard words the grownups have to dish out. I lay back on my bed, thinking madly, "I'll just take my good old time. She can't make me clean my room any faster than I want."

I lay there and thought about the lousy week at school.

It was the gym class that got to me first. I've got a coach who's a "Yeah, rah, rah, team effort" sort. He's always on my back becuase I can't measure up in volleyball. It's height that matters there. All I ever hear in gym period is "Jump up there, Carey, sock that ball! Move it!" Trying doesn't count. And there's always a taller kid who smacks the ball from right in front of me. "You gotta grow a little, Carey," the coach says to me on Thursday, right in front of all the guys. Some of them turned away and snickered. As if I don't want to grow! As if I was somehow keeping myself short to bug the coach!

When I got back to the locker room, my lunch money was gone from my locker. Lots of kids have money and things hooked from their lockers during gym class. There's no way to find out who's taken it, much less get it back. The office won't loan money to kids in the junior high. Usually you can borrow from a friend who's flush, but after class I didn't feel much like asking one of the guys for a loan. I was hungry, and I didn't want to miss lunch that day, so I asked one of the lunchroom aides if I could borrow 35¢ from her. She was real nice about it, and I told her I'd pay her back the next day.

Well, that was Thursday. I told Mom what had happened, and she gave me the 70¢ to take on Friday. She told me to see if I could leave the money in the office until lunchtime, to make sure it would be there to pay the lunch aide back. "And be sure to ask for a receipt, Jonathan," Mom said. She's strict about that, ever since the man at the corner grocery stopped me once and accused me of stealing a candy bar that I'd bought at another store. "Kids are always suspect," Mom had said then. "You protect yourself by always getting your receipt and keeping it with you."

So that morning I took my 70¢ to the office and waited around and waited around with a bunch of other kids who were bringing notes and stuff. Finally the woman got to me, and I gave her my money to keep. She said okay, and then I said, "Could I have a receipt, please?" I guess she didn't hear me at first, she had already turned away. Then she saw me still standing there and she asked, "What are you waiting for?" in a kind of irritated way. I said, "I'd like a receipt for my money." She got all red and shoved my 70¢ back at me and yelled, "All right, then! Keep it yourself!" Right in front of all those kids and everyone. I hated her. I could have socked her. I thought I'd die. Right in front of everybody, she acted as if I were a criminal.

I couldn't forget it all day long, her yelling at me like that just because I'd asked for a receipt. I kept my mouth shut in every class. I'm usually one of the first to speak up, but it seemed like every teacher I had sounded like that woman in the office. All day the teachers kept reminding me of that woman shoving my money back and yelling at me. Grownups are supposed to be shown respect, but they sure don't show any respect for kids!

Remembering it all in my room, I was still hopping mad. "Grownups are all alike—teachers and parents, too," I thought. I considered not cleaning my room at all, just staying down there and missing supper. But then I remembered that Mom had said I could go downtown shopping Saturday. I'd saved my money for a record I wanted, and if I didn't clean my room she'd be still mad and I couldn't go. I got up and started cleaning—slowly. It seemed like grownups had the upper hand no matter which way you turned.

I didn't buy my record the next day. It wasn't any different from school no matter where a kid went. At the record store I stood around and stood around and stood around waiting for the salesman to wait on me, and every time I got up to the counter some grownups shoved up, too. They were always waited on first. I stood on tiptoe till my toes ached, trying to stretch myself taller. That guy behind the counter just seemed to look right through me and at the big people.

I was turning to give up and go when I noticed the salesman was arguing with someone. I looked around and heard him say, "I can't give you an exchange on this. It was on sale and sold 'as is.'" I heard a woman say in a soft way, "But I found it was warped when I took it out of the jacket." Her back was to me, but I could see the salesman's face. He had an ugly little smile. "What'd you do? Lay it on top of a radiator?" The woman sucked in her breath, then said, "It was warped when I brought it home. I have my receipt right here." The salesman said, hard, "I can't help you!"

I watched the woman turn and go, and then I left the store in a hurry. Outside the sidewalks were wet, it was raining again. The air was cold and I kept my head down and watched my feet make splatters on the wet cement. That salesman had treated that woman just like a kid. And she was grown up. I didn't like to think about it, and I walked faster. "It's a tough world." My mom's words came back in my mind, and I could see her standing there in my bedroom looking not only mad, but tired, too. "Why don't you wax floors in the morning?" I could hear myself saying that to her, and it was all mixed up in my mind with that salesman's ugly smile.

I ducked into the refreshment bar at Woolworth's for a hot dog before hopping a bus home—suddenly I wanted to get home. Woolworth's was crowded like it always is. I started to elbow my way through a bunch of kids my age and a little older. Then I noticed a kid maybe eight or nine. His coat was damp and his hair still wet with rain. He had money clutched in his hand. He was trying to push his way into the crowd towards the hot dogs. Something in his face reminded me all over again of the woman at the record counter.

Suddenly I got mad. I reached out and grabbed the little kid's hand and started shoving the big kids. I kept yelling, "Hey you guys! Move over! This kid was here first!" They looked around and down at him, and then a few moved back and made room. He put his money firmly on the counter and said to the girl, "A hot dog and Coke, please." He gave me a funny look, like he was wondering how come I'd bothered to help him. Just then my bus came. I raced for the door and caught it just before it moved away from the curb.

I grabbed a seat in the back, and thought about that little kid looking up at me. I couldn't help grinning. Suddenly I felt pretty good. I sat up straight and looked out the window at the rain and all the people hurrying, hurrying. "It's a good day to clean the garage," I thought. I couldn't wait to get home. I could almost see Mom smile.

Note

Now is an appropriate time to meet with others in a group to share the results of the exercises in this chapter and to assist each other in refining understanding and skills.

Before you meet, though, read the directions for the next activity, "Preparing for Laboratory Experience," and be prepared to participate in that sharing activity.

ACTIVITIES: PREPARING FOR LABORATORY EXPERIENCE

Directions

1. Design, and refine, a question sequence for interpreting a story you have selected. Use "Instructional Plan: Interpreting a Story" and "Criteria for Success" (below) to help you guide your planning.
    a. Read the story carefully.
    b. Determine the content focus. The discussion should have a *purpose*. It should lead toward an *objective* determined in advance: Do you want

the students ultimately to state a *generalization,* a set of *values, personal feelings,* or a *scientific* idea?

    c.   Design a question sequence that builds logically to the expression of the objective. Use the outline "Interpreting, Basic Question Strategy," on pages 81–83, to assist you in designing the discussion.

    d.   With colleagues, role-play the sequence as teacher and students.

    e.   Refine the sequence.

2.   Review "Procedure for Lab Experiences" and "Directions for Taping a Lesson," pages 66–68.

3.   As soon as possible, conduct and tape-record the laboratory experience and analyze the results as directed in "Analysis of Laboratory Experience" (pages 69–70).

Instructional Plan: Interpreting a Story

Content Focus

Material:_____

Purpose:_____

_____

_____

_____

Question Sequence

1. Open Describing Question: _____

_____

_____

2. Closed Describing Questions: _____

_____

_____

_____

3. Explaining Questions: _____

_____

_____

_____

4. Potential Testing Questions: _____

_____

_____

_____

_____

Criteria for Success for a Laboratory Experience

The following criteria should be used in judging the level of competency demonstrated in your laboratory experience.

1. The *content focus,* as stated in the "Instructional Plan," identifies the story and describes in report language the *objective* of the discussion.

2. Questions asked accurately illustrate the language action called for in each category: open describing, closed describing, explaining, and testing.

3. Students' explanations are not judged by means of highly judgmental words (good, excellent, right, wrong); instead, the teacher either:
    a. Accepts the statement with a comment of "I see," "I understand," or "That's interesting."
    b. Asks a predicting or explaining question to help the student test the usefulness of her or his idea.

4. An attempt is made to determine the personal meaning of highly inferential-judgmental words by asking for personal meaning, asking for an illustration, or paraphrasing.

5. Psychological support is supplied when students seem to need it: "Take your time." "Would you like to think about it for a few minutes?" "Mistakes are part of learning, aren't they?"

ACTIVITIES: ANALYSIS OF LABORATORY EXPERIENCE

Directions

As soon as possible after completion of the laboratory experience:

1. Refer to the Data Collection Guide (page 107).

2. Listen to your tape and record the information requested on the guide. Be certain to record the questions exactly as you asked them—not as you *intended* to ask them. Play the tape as many times as necessary to record the required data.

3. Examine each question carefully to determine if it accurately fits the intended category type. Code each question as:

> OD—Open describing
> CD—Closed describing
> E—Explaining
> P—Predicting

If you have difficulty discriminating, reread Chapter 3, "Language Actions." Attempt to be as accurate as possible in your discrimination.

If the questions asked do not accurately fit the category type called for on the Data Collection Guide, refine them, or design new questions, which do fit.

4. Note the *objective* of the lesson and examine the interaction to determine the extent to which the objective was achieved. Attempt to determine the *cause* of whatever degree of achievement was obtained.

5. Examine the data for judgmental statements, supportive statements, and attempts to determine personal meaning. You may wish to listen to the tape again to analyze the circumstances as they occurred.

    a. If you expressed a judgment of the student's explanations, *how could you have avoided it?* You may, at this point, still be having difficulty accepting the teacher behavior of responding to students' explanations without judging them. After all, you have gone through your entire life expecting to have your ideas judged for truthfulness and accuracy by others. But the fact remains—and it is worth repeating once more—that the interpreting, inquiry, and knowledge-generating and testing process depends on students having the skill and the opportunity to test the accuracy, degree of truthfulness, and effectiveness of their own ideas.

    b. If a student used an inferential-judgmental word:

        (1) Did you attempt to determine personal meaning?

        (2) If so, was the probe effective? How might it have been more effective?

        (3) If not, how best might the personal meaning have been determined?

    c. Did you use statements that provided psychological support? Did you use any statements that in any way put the student(s) down? If you used negative statements, how could they have been avoided?

6. When you have completed the analysis, record those specific things you would do differently next time. You may feel it is advisable to schedule another lab experience at this point to refine your understanding and skill.

Data Collection Guide for Laboratory Experience

Name _____ Date _____

Classroom Teacher's Name _____ School_____

Grade Level _____ Number of Students _____

Directions

1. *Content Focus*
   Indicate the name of the story and the objective of the discussion.

2. *Development of Lesson*
   a. Using the chart below, record in sequence the questions you asked and the first student response to each question. Code the language action of each question: OD, CD, E, P, or C.
   b. Record any instances of the following in the *teacher* column. Record them as they occur in the discussion sequence and identify each with a brief label: highly judgmental statements, psychologically supporting statements, and psychologically rejecting statements.
   c. Record in the *student* column any student statement or behavior you feel is significant in relation to the outcome of the lesson.

Teacher	Students

Source Notes

1. Fred E. Newton, *Facilitating Inquiry in the Classroom* (Portland, Oreg.: Northwest Regional Educational Laboratory, 1970), p. 88.

2. Tohr Yamaguchi, *The Golden Crane* (New York: Holt, Rinehart and Winston, 1963). Reprinted by permission.

3. *New York Times,* October 28, 1961, © 1961 by The New York Times Company. Reprinted by permission.

4. Yamaguchi, op. cit.

5. John A. McCollum and Rose Marie Davis, *Instructor's Manual: Development of Higher Level Thinking Abilities* (Portland, Oreg.: Northwest Regional Educational Laboratory, 1972).

6. Bonnie Smith Yackel, "It's a Tough World," in *Identity* (Minneapolis: Winston Press/ Mime Publications, 1972).

5 *Fact or Fantasy?*

Overview

Rationale

The effectiveness of an idea generated by a student in the inquiry process is contingent upon the degree to which the student personally feels that the idea will explain why something exists or performs in a particular way or the degree to which she or he feels the idea can be used to predict the consequences of similar situations. In other words, the meaning or usefulness or value of the idea is a personal thing—truth, right, and good are in the student's head, based on the extent to which the idea has been tested. Consequently, the most important strategy for the teaching process of inquiry is the teaching behavior of facilitating students *testing* the usefulness of ideas. The emphasis in this chapter is on developing a set of teaching strategies to conduct that testing process.

General Objectives

The material in this chapter is designed to create the conditions by which you will develop:

- Sensitivity to the importance of providing students with information sources as close to the event or phenomenon being considered as possible.

- An understanding that knowledge is relative—that there is no such thing as absolute truth or a completely right answer.

- The ability to discriminate between sources of information with respect to the degree to which the data represent the event or phenomenon itself.

- The behavior of describing sources when providing data.

- The behavior of including words that connote tentativeness of knowledge and avoiding words that connote absolute truth when giving an explanation.

- The behavior of avoiding judgmental terms when responding to students' ideas.

- The behavior of responding to students' ideas by asking them to test the ideas.

At the conclusion of this chapter you should have the understanding and skill to design and implement a lesson that results in students analyzing a body of specific data, verbalizing personal interpretations (explanations of causal relationships), and testing those interpretations for validity and/or reliability.

Searching for the Real World

Successful implementation of the inquiry process requires that both the teacher and the students clearly perceive the extent to which the considered data represent the real world. The power of any idea is evident in the degree to which it can be used as a basis for explaining the present and predicting and controlling the future. An interpretation based on direct and personal observations and measurements is likely to be far more meaningful and useful than an interpretation based on the statements of a teacher who lectures on the propositions of an author who is interpreting what another individual has observed and described. Consequently, in the knowledge-generating and testing process, the information on which the ideas are based needs to be as close to reality as possible—and when it is not, students need to be aware of the extent to which it is not. If they are given the impression that "truth" lies within the teacher and/or the textbook, the process becomes some sort of meaningless, insane game of trying to guess what the teacher considers to be right or wrong, good or bad, rather than what works or is useful in explaining reality. Yet, to a great degree, such a game seems to be the pattern in many classrooms. In classrooms where a series of textbooks is the basic data source, it is not uncommon to hear the following kinds of statements: "All right, let's stick to the facts." "What facts were you able to obtain?" "The fact of the matter is. . . ." All of these statements sound logical, but the problem is, What is a fact? Wendell Johnson has identified four basic assumptions that must be taken into account in order to answer that question.[1]

1. *A fact is necessarily incomplete. There are definite limitations to our ability to observe the world about us, to say nothing of our ability to observe ourselves. In order to sense beyond certain limits, we must use instruments such as the microscope, and even they have their limitations. In other words, we get only as much of the facts as we can with the sensory organs—and the magnifying devices—we have to work with. Thus, . . . inescapably, in our endeavor to understand reality we are somewhat like a man trying to understand the mechanism of a closed watch which he has no way of opening. So far we may go and no farther in our explorations of reality. Our "facts" are incomplete.*

2. *Facts change. Facts as we observe them are little more than quick glimpses of a ceaseless transformation—as if we viewed the separate frames of a moving picture without quite realizing that what we were viewing was, in fact, a moving picture. Looking closely at a motion-picture film we see that each successive frame is slightly different from the last. Just so, looking closely at a fact we see*

FACT OR FANTASY?

that it appears slightly — or markedly — different from time to time. . . . A person, as we know him, is a kind of average, a fusion or blending, an abstract of many different observations that we have made of him. Each observation occurs only once, and each fact observed is unique. What is important to remain aware of is the "fact" of change itself — the facts that we observe are in a constant process of change.

3. *A fact is a personal affair.* In a basic sense, a fact is an observation. An observation is the act of an individual. That is why a fact (a personal observation) is necessarily incomplete — the person who observes it is limited in his observational capacity. This same condition helps to explain why a fact changes: the individual who observes it is always changing — he observes differently each time he observes. The world as we know it is a joint product of the observer and the observed. A number of studies have demonstrated that no two individuals observe or sense a situation in exactly the same manner. This is true of all of our sensory modes, with individual differences becoming tremendously more varied as a result of the conditioning processes accompanying natural growth. Consequently, a fact, as an observation, is a personal affair, to be trusted as such and not as a universal truth.

4. *A fact is useful, or dependable, to the degree that other persons agree with you concerning it.* If the majority say something is green every time you say it is red, you had best take their word for it. If a doctor, two interns, and a nurse all agree that there are no grasshoppers on your suit jacket, you might as well quit trying to brush them off. Generally speaking, the larger the number of people who agree as to a fact, the more dependable the fact is. Given that observations are made under similar conditions (equal availability of sensory instruments, for example) by individuals who have demonstrated reliability in their observations, we can generally say a fact is a fact when the majority agree concerning it. However, there is the problem of inner experience which is observed by one and cannot be verified by another. For example, pains, itches, fears, or anxieties, which cannot be directly observed by a second person, may be (a) reliable, (b) deliberately false, or (c) hysterical. Only by indirect evidence can we attempt to determine which description is correct. We accept it as reliable when it is consistent with the conditions and the behavior associated with it. Whether, or to what degree, it is consistent, and so reliable, depends, even in this case, on agreement among the persons who are in a position to observe its consistency.

Therefore, we may say a "fact" is an observation agreed upon by two or more persons situated, qualified, and equipped to make it — and the more persons agreeing, the better.

Implications for the Classroom

If we recognize that the "accuracy" of data is always subject to question — that the world is in a constant process of change, that new knowledge is constantly being generated, modifying and invalidating the old—then it seems obvious that in the classroom both the teacher and the students must realize there are no absolutes, or absolute truths, or completely right answers of the kind so often implied by the interaction between teachers and students. There is evidence that indicates that early in children's school experience they no longer see the classroom as a place where they can generate meanings of the world for themselves but as a place where they seek meaning—the meaning being the teacher's, the textbook's, the authority's.

Neil Postman and Charles Weingartner have taken a cue from Ernest Hemingway, whom they quote as having replied, when asked if he believed there was an essential ingredient required to be a great writer, answered, "Yes, there is. In order to be a great writer a person must have a built-in, shockproof crap detector."[2]

It seems to us that, in his response, Hemingway identified an essential strategy and the essential function of the schools in today's world. One way of looking at the history of the human group is that it has been a continuing struggle against the veneration of "crap." Our intellectual history is a chronicle of anguish and suffering of men who tried to help their contemporaries see that some part of their fondest beliefs were misconceptions, faulty assumptions, superstitions, and even outright lies. The mileposts along the road of our intellectual development signal those points at which some person developed a perspective, a new meaning, or a new metaphor. We have in mind a new education that would set out to cultivate just such people— experts at "crap detecting."[3]

The tragedy of allowing (and sometimes even encouraging) children to believe that what they read is a completely accurate and final description of the real world is that we prepare them to live in a world that does not exist. Postman and Weingartner use the term *future shock* to describe the results:

Future shock occurs when you are confronted by the fact that the world you were educated to believe in doesn't exist. Your images of reality are apparitions that disappear on contact. There are several ways of responding to such a condition, one of which is to withdraw and allow oneself to be overcome by a sense of impotence. More commonly, one continues to act as if his apparitions were substantial— relentlessly pursuing a course of action that he knows will fail him.[4]

In other words, treating interpretations of the world as though they represented, with perfect fidelity, the world itself must inevitably result in some degree of malfunctioning. A metaphor used by general semanticists expresses the same idea in terms of *map and territory*. S. I. Hayakawa develops that metaphor in the following passage:

If a child grows to adulthood with a verbal world in his head which corresponds fairly closely to the real world that he finds around him in his widening experience, he is in relatively small danger of being shocked or hurt by what he finds because his verbal world has told him what, more or less, to expect. He is prepared for life. If, however, he grows up with a false map in his head—that is, with a head crammed with false knowledge and superstition — he will constantly be running into trouble, wasting his efforts, and acting like a fool. He will not be adjusted to the world as it is; he may, if the lack of adjustment is serious, end up in a mental hospital.[5]

Ironically, one of the places where children often get inadequate maps is the classroom. This is so not because schools deliberately dispense false information but because pupils are so often allowed or encouraged to regard teachers and textbooks as sources of truth or of factual knowledge. Instead of developing a healthy skepticism toward the interpretations that help them form verbal maps, the pupils often become naively trusting of any proposition that appears in print, or that is uttered by an authority figure. Such propositions go unquestioned into their maps, even though they may be vastly remote from experienced reality which is the source of factual knowledge. Most textbooks, for example (unless they are scientific journal accounts) are about as far from the event or phenomenon — the ultimate source of facts — as any available medium of information can possibly be. The remoteness of any print medium becomes evident when one examines what happens to a news report before it is finally published in the local paper. Undoubtedly most thinking adults recognize that a news article represents the reporter's interpretation of the event being reported. However, few people realize the number of interpretations that modify the report before it is finally published.

Chart 5-1 indicates the numbers of individuals who influence a report of a foreign event.[6] Each of them unquestionably has unique background experiences, values, biases, and styles that modify the content, and hence the effect, at each successive step. It is instructive to bear in mind, while examining the figure, that textbook statements are typically separated from events by many additional layers of process and interpretation. The text writer might well *begin* his or her interpretive process from the report printed in the *New York Times*.

The problem of recognizing and dealing objectively with the real world becomes ever more difficult as the event being considered withdraws farther and farther into the obscurity of historical distance. Edwin Fenton states a strong case for students developing the skill of interpreting historical interpretations:

History is really a way of reading and writing about events in the past. Since only a tiny proportion of all the events that have happened were recorded and saved for posterity, history cannot be an accurate record of everything in the past. Moreover, no historian in a single lifetime could read all the extant material on a topic as complicated, for example, as the Protestant Reformation. Hence, history is not even an accurate record of all the information about the past. In addition, the historian doing research selects from the mass of material that he reads those pieces of information which seem to him significant. What seems significant is conditioned by a man's conception of the nature of causation and by his personal characteristics and experiences. The very act of selecting evidence implies interpretation.

This argument leads to the conclusion that we must teach methods of interpretation if we claim to teach history. Students must learn the rules by which historians collect evidence and use it to interpret the past if they are to read or write

CHART 5-1

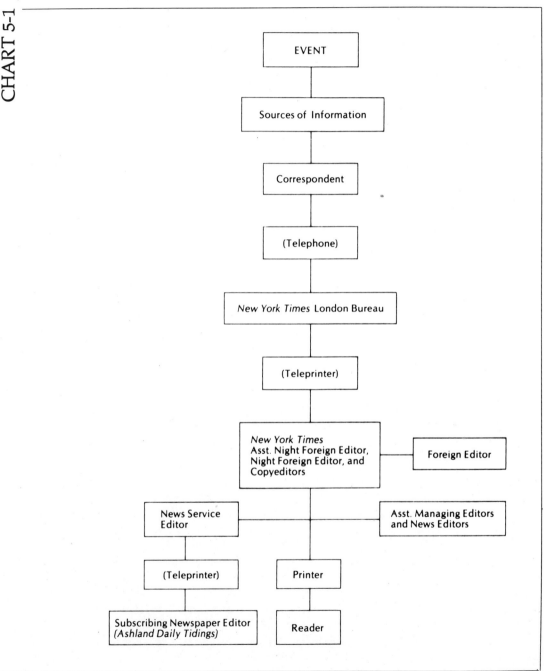

EVENT

Sources of Information

Correspondent

(Telephone)

New York Times London Bureau

(Teleprinter)

New York Times
Asst. Night Foreign Editor,
Night Foreign Editor, and
Copyeditors

Foreign Editor

News Service
Editor

Asst. Managing Editors
and News Editors

(Teleprinter)

Printer

Subscribing Newspaper Editor
(Ashland Daily Tidings)

Reader

history intelligently. They must be able to judge whether an author's conclusions are supported by the evidence on which these conclusions are based. Unless students are taught to interpret, they are not taught history at all. Teaching the mode of inquiry of history and the social sciences lies at the heart of the new social studies.[7]

It is for these reasons that teachers must be well aware just how closely the information they are using to facilitate meaning making in the classroom corresponds to the reality of pertinent events and phenomena. The following behaviors are specific techniques that help students generate and test meanings of reality for themselves.

Teaching Behaviors*

1. *When students are asked to engage in the knowledge-generating and testing process, data as close as possible to the reality of the event or phenomenon being considered are provided.* Both teacher and students need to be clearly aware of the source of the data used as the basis for an explanation, and the extent to which the data represent the actual event or phenomenon being considered.

   Generally, data are available to students through the following sources (arranged according to increasing remoteness):

   a. Seeing, smelling, touching, tasting, hearing by direct sensory contact as well as through reliable extensions of the senses, such as scientific instruments—observing events or phenomena, as they occur naturally, or as they are demonstrated for the purposes of observation.

   b. Viewing motion pictures, hearing tape recordings—experiencing representations of the actual event that have a high degree of completeness, objectivity, and fidelity.

   c. Viewing still photos of the event—examining artifacts or paraphernalia directly involved in the event.

   d. Listening to and questioning another who was there and who is now referring to his or her written record of the event.

   e. Reading original documents such as letters, diaries, journals (particularly scientific journals), and so on, prepared by individuals who were there.

   f. Reading text materials based on documents, written reports, and photos prepared by another person (textbooks).

   g. Listening to someone tell what he or she has abstracted from text materials (the usual lecture).

---

* The behaviors presented here are adapted from unpublished materials developed by the Northwest Regional Educational Laboratory, Portland, Oreg.

To a great extent, the *source* of the data indicates the strength of the idea. Generally, reporting that the idea being expressed is based on direct, personal observation gives it much greater credibility than indicating that the idea is based on the writings of someone who interpreted the diary statements of the grandson of the man who was there.

2. *When providing data, the teacher describes and qualifies the source of data.* When the teacher provides information for students to consider as a basis for generating ideas, the information is not presented in a way that makes it seem unquestionably authoritative or factual in nature and the students are not left to guess the source of the data. Information is presented in a manner that indicates the source and, if possible, qualifies the source's reliability:

"I observed after repeating the experiment several times that . . ."

"According to our text, whose author lived for many years in the West Indies, . . ."

"A reporter for *Time* magazine, who had interviewed Dr. Kissinger, wrote . . ."

"I have never been to Chicago, but it seems to me that . . ."

3. *When the teacher states an explanation, words connoting the tentativeness of knowledge will be included. Words connoting "absolute truth" will be avoided.* A behavior that occurs in most classrooms where the principal sources of data are the teacher and the textbook is that of overgeneralizing. Both the teacher and the students are prone to use words that connote absolute cause. For example:

Caused: **"Increasing heat** *caused* **the liquid to boil."**

Resulted: **"His desire for justice** *resulted* **in unlawful behavior."**

Determined: **"Cultural patterns are** *determined* **by environment."**

Such statements create reality problems for the simple reason that at most they are only partially true, never *absolutely* true, and sometimes just plain untrue. Consequently, it is important to recognize the need to use words that indicate clearly the tentative nature of knowledge. For example:

"One **cause of . . ."**

". . . helped to produce . . ."

"One **reason for the result was . . ."**

Also, note that the following words connote *cause* but, because they also connote *tentativeness,* they are more helpful in explaining the real world:

Facilitate: **"The discovery of the transistor** *facilitated* **the development of computers."**

FACT OR FANTASY?

Affect: **"Sunstorms** *affect* **radio transmission."**

Influence: **"Where people live** *often influences* **how they live."**

Notice in the last statement two words that connote the tentativeness of knowledge, *often* and *influences*. Also note how much more powerful and effective this statement is in explaining the real world or predicting a new event than an absolute statement such as "Culture is determined by environment." For one thing, the latter statement totally ignores technological control of environment and is therefore only partially useful.

4.   *When a student states an explanation as an absolute truth, the teacher will ask him or her to consider:*

    a.   The extent to which that explanation is useful in accounting for other situations *(testing validity),* or

    b.   The extent to which that explanation can be used as a basis for predicting the consequences of a future event *(testing reliability).*

        The term *validity* here means the degree to which the idea is *useful in accounting for other situations.* "Is it a *valid* explanation? Can it account for other, parallel or comparable situations?"

        The term *reliability* here expresses the degree to which the idea is *useful* in *predicting* future situations. "To what degree is the idea likely to consistently explain parallel or comparable situations?"

        Examples of the behavior are:

Student: **"The political policies in Latin America are based on religious influences."**

Teacher: **"To what extent does that explain the election of a Communist Party candidate in Chile?"** or **"Based on that explanation, could you predict that only candidates with strong religious affiliations will be elected next month?"**

The intent here is to help students judge for themselves the extent to which their ideas are useful. The teacher is taken out of the ridiculous authority role of pronouncing judgments of right or wrong on every student-generated idea. Instead, he or she helps students to develop and test their own meanings of reality.

5.   *When a student is engaged in the knowledge-generating and testing process, the teacher will not judge explanations as good, bad, right, wrong, excellent idea, right-on, or by using any other strongly affective terms.*

        In order to generate an explanation, data must be available on which the idea can be based. It is at that level—the level of *describing data*—that judging is appropriate and necessary. At the level of data description, it is appropriate for the teacher to say in advance:

"Class, we will need to have information as accurate as possible, so let's all report any differences between what we have personally observed and what is reported by others."

At this point, it is also legitimate for the teacher to correct a student by saying, for example:

"Bill, our book says that ice freezes at 32° Fahrenheit at sea level, not 32° Celsius."

However, if you want students to generate and test *explanations* for themselves, you *must allow this autonomy to occur.* When a student generates an explanation, no matter how strong or weak, useful or ineffectual the explanation may seem to be, your role is to help the student judge the idea for herself or himself.*

The teaching behavior called for is to ask the student to consider:

a.   the extent to which the explanation is useful in accounting for other situations, or

b.   the extent to which the explanation can be used as a basis for predicting the consequences of a future event.

EXERCISE: CONTENT FOCUS

Both teachers and students need to be aware of the extent to which the data considered represent the real world. This exercise will help you in selecting a lesson topic and identifying a series of important data sources that match specified types and levels of information. It is important to be sensitive to the *content focus* of your lesson topic. Content focus here means an area of the curriculum that serves as the subject of an instructional sequence or lesson. Generally, a content focus is stated in one of three ways:

1.   *A general topic.* Examples are: "Alaska," "The Lumber Industry," "The Short Story," "Simple Machines," "The Commutative Law for Multiplication," and so on.

2.   *A specific event.* A phenomenon described in relation to time, space, condition, actions, and/or interactions. Examples are: "The internal political problems of Kenya during the first year of its independence." "The effect of

---

*   Again, this behavior is in direct opposition to that advocated by behavior modification theorists. If you are having difficulty with the idea that the student, rather than the teacher, should judge the usefulness of student-generated ideas, you should refer again to Chart 1-1 on page 8. To be able to facilitate this teaching behavior effectively, I really think you have to come to grips with the decision of whether you wish to promote behaviorism or humanism in your classroom.

controlled amounts of water and light on lima beans planted under otherwise similar conditions in room 17, Andersonville Elementary School."

3. *A generalization.* An explanation statement summarizing the cause-and-effect relationship between concepts being considered. Examples are: "The development of farm technology has had a marked effect on farm products, farm income, and farm population." "Water, chemical action, and living things are important in the splitting and breaking down of rocks."

A thoughtful comparison of the three types of content focus statements should convince you that either of the two latter types will be much more useful for designing an instructional sequence than will the first type. General topics are nearly always too broad, ambiguous, and ill-defined to be very helpful in providing structure for a lesson.

Directions

Discriminate among the various types of content focus statements by coding each of the following statements as

T—General *topic*

E—Specific *event*

G—*Generalization*

_____ 1. The development of the printing press promoted increased literacy throughout the world.

_____ 2. The history of Western civilization.

_____ 3. Economic specialization helps to produce a higher standard of living.

_____ 4. The hunting experiences of an Eskimo family in Greenland during the winter of 1964.

_____ 5. Keeping a journal of day-to-day personal experiences has a positive effect on the ability to express ideas.

_____ 6. The literature of Henry David Thoreau.

_____ 7. Results obtained by students in a fifth-grade class, using selected simple machines in a controlled manner to move specified objects a measured distance.

Answers and Explanations

__G__ 1. *A generalization.* The content focus is expressed in the form of an *explanation* statement.

__T__ 2. A general *topic.* The content focus is very broad and very ambiguous.

_____ G _ 3. Another *generalization.* An explanation statement of a cause-and-effect relationship.

_____ E _ 4. A specific *event.* A phenomenon stated in terms of time, space, conditions, actions, and interactions.

_____ G _ 5. *Generalization.* Again, a cause-and-effect explanation statement.

_____ T _ 6. A general *topic* of information.

_____ E _ 7. An *event,* described in terms of time, space, conditions, actions, and interactions.

   If you had difficulty discriminating among the three forms, (1) review the exercise, (2) practice making up examples of each of the three forms, and (3) ask colleagues for their assistance and/or schedule a conference with your instructor.

ACTIVITIES: SOURCES OF DATA

Directions

   Use the following worksheet to record your responses to the instructions below.

1. Select and state a content focus at the grade level and in the subject matter area of your choice. The content focus should be either an event or a generalization.

2. Design an introductory activity that sets the purpose of the lesson and motivates students to become interested and involved. For example, a primary school teacher, introducing a lesson dealing with the effect of earthworms on soil, simply placed a worm on each pupil's desk with the direction to observe as many things as possible in the next five minutes. A junior high school social studies teacher introduced a unit on emerging African nations by presenting a vocabulary list of important social, economic, and political terms relating to a particular African nation, plus a series of pictures portraying events occurring in that nation. The class was organized into small groups with the task set by the direction, "Come up with as many ideas as you can of what you would expect to find if you had the opportunity to visit this country next week."

3. Identify a series of data sources that, to the extent possible for the content being considered, match the categories indicated. Do not be concerned with identifying specific titles of books, films, and so on. However, describe rather specifically the type of activity or material you might use for each level. For example, a motion picture that presents the relationship between the environment and how people live.

FACT OR FANTASY?

Worksheet: Sources of Data

1. Content focus: _____

_____

2. Introductory activity:_____

_____

_____

3. Data sources:

		Category	Source
	a.	Direct involvement to observe personally, record, and measure. Participation in the event or process itself.	
	b.	Demonstration of the actual event for student observation without direct participation.	
	c.	Motion picture or tape-recording of the actual event.	
	d.	Still photos or artifacts of the event itself.	
	e.	Verbal interaction with another person who has been directly in-volved in the event itself.	
	f.	Original documents prepared by individuals who participated in the event (especially scientific journals).	
	g.	Text materials (interpretations of the event by individuals who were not there).	
	h.	Listening to what someone has extracted from text materials.	

ACTIVITIES: ANALYSIS OF A DISCUSSION OF THE U-2 INCIDENT

This discussion provides an opportunity to develop a growing awareness of types and levels of data, and strategies for the effective use of the process of interpreting data.

Directions

First, read the discussion, then answer the questions that follow it. Each comment in the discussion has been numbered in sequence. When appropriate, cite numbers to indicate the evidence that supports your response. Be prepared to share your responses at your next group session.

Following is a current events discussion in a junior high school classroom shortly after the appearance of news headlines and stories of a plane being shot down over Russia, "the U-2 incident."

(1) Teacher: "This morning during activity class, many of you wondered if I had seen the headline in the paper this morning. This was again about the plane that had been shot down over Russia. Now Sandra was wondering just how this plane got into Russia in the first place."

(2) Sandra: "Well, I just can't understand how after all the warfare and all of the things that we've been learning about, Russia is so advanced above us and here this plane got into Russia a couple of thousand miles and they didn't see it. Of course, it did get shot down, but I just can't understand with all their warfare how it did get in there."

(3) Jerry: "Well, I could say that brightens our hopes for retaliation, if they do attack us, but I wonder if they didn't purposely let the plane get in there so they could have an undisputed claim that we were spying on them. After all the little border incidents like some of them have been, I don't know if those were spying missions or not but they, ah, someone's always been able to talk their way out of it. So they possibly let the plane get in there in order so they could have a foolproof case on us."

(4) Teacher: "Now Jerry's mentioned that. That perhaps the Russians allowed this plane to get in there deliberately so that they might have an edge of some type on us in the propaganda war that is going on in the world today. Ah, now this is of particular importance today because of the summit conference that is beginning now. Marci, you were reading about the summit conference last week. Of what importance is this and the plane incident?"

(5) Marci: "Well, they'll probably discuss it and they'll think something's, well, that Russia is trying to, oh, get above us in some way and they're trying to get, they're trying to let the plane get into the country so they could shoot it down. This could start a third world war."

(6) Teacher: "All right, now are there any other thoughts on this plane incident? Bill?"

FACT OR FANTASY?

(7) Bill: "Well, there was some discussion on whether it, the plane, had mechanical difficulty or . . ."

(8) Teacher: "Now, this is a good point now, go ahead."

(9) Bill: "Or whether it was shot down. And the Russians also said that they had the plane in about one piece."

(10) Teacher: "Um hm."

(11) Bill: "I don't see how they could have had it in one piece when it was, ah, it fell from 65,000 feet in the air."

(12) Teacher: "I see."

(13) Bill: "And they said they were so far advanced in missile warfare and everything like that, so how could the plane have gotten so far into Russian territory?"

(14) Teacher: "Um hm."

(15) Sarah: "And, ah, they, there is also some things they said that, they probably, ah, they're probably going to shoot the, the pilot and well, I don't think that's the right thing to do, they should settle it peaceably and discuss it, and."

(16) Teacher: "All right. Sandra, you have your hand up. What point did you wish to add?"

(17) Sandra: "Well, maybe um, that man, I don't remember his name right now, is it Powell?"

(18) Teacher: "Who can recall the pilot's name now? Marcia?"

(19) Marcia: "I wouldn't know."

(20) Teacher: "Susan?"

(21) Susan: "Powers."

(22) Teacher: "Powers, that's right."

(23) Sandra: "Well, this Mr. Powers, maybe he went in there on purpose. Instead of working with us maybe he was working with the Russians and maybe he was an agent of some type who went in there on purpose and, and brought all this stuff in there and got so far in and, and made everything plain and, and so that everyone would be suspicious of the United States and what exactly they were doing."

(24) Teacher: "Um hm. Now this is a good point. Are there any other thoughts on this? Karen?"

(25) Karen: "Well, do they know who sent the man into Russia?"

(26) Teacher: "Does anyone know now who gave the orders, do you recall this from your newspaper readings?"

(27) Bill: "Secretary Herter said that he wasn't going to, Secretary of State Herter said that he wasn't going to reveal who sent him in, but they do know that the United States didn't tell him to go."

(28) Teacher: "Well, now the big question seems to be should we have sent this pilot in the first place? Robert?"

(29) Robert: "Um, I don't think he should have gone through the right channels, I'm not sure he got permission from high enough to go in. Ah, he—I know this sounds kind of way out, but he could've gotten permission, he was going on a

short flight taking the plane somewhere or another for repairs and had the mechanical difficulty in there after he had sort of snuck into Russia, and just by luck had not gotten shot down.''

(30) Teacher: ''All right, now this is a good point, Robert has mentioned the mechanical difficulty now. Any other thoughts? Sharon?''

(31) Sharon: ''Well, even if the plane did have a mechanical difficulty, if we tried to impress that upon the Russians they wouldn't believe us because they are trying to find something against us.''

(32) Teacher: ''Karen.''

(33) Karen: ''Do you think the United States would have done the same thing if there was a Russian ship or a Russian plane?''

(34) Teacher: ''All right. Now Karen has asked a question. Now what would the United States have done in such an instance? Kim?''

(35) Kim: ''Well, I think that maybe they would have, well, that's the way the Russians did it. I think they probably should have because if Russia wants to be, doesn't want American planes flying over it and finding out different things about her country, then . . .''

(Tape goes off)

(36) Teacher: ''All right, now we've heard several different opinions of this problem of the Russian plane, so let's recall the several items that have been mentioned. Sharon, would you just briefly tell us now what has been mentioned so far so we can get all of the thoughts together?''

(37) Sharon: ''Well, we don't know whether it was mechanical difficulty or shot down, the reason the plane came down. And we don't know whether the man was sent by one of our officials to go over there or whether he did it purposely or whether it was for some other reason.''

(38) Teacher: ''Any other thoughts on this? Sandra?''

(39) Sandra: ''Well, I'd like to know why in the world, I mean he would just go in there. I mean it's so—someone would be so scared, because he knew it was fatal death. I mean, he just couldn't go all the way across Russia and not someone see him with all those difficulties and things like that. What kind of things do they have in that plane that they wanted so much? I mean what did he have in there? Did he have anything that he could shoot back at them or something?''

(40) Teacher: ''Well, now Sandra's brought up a very good point, what type of information do you think this aircraft would be seeking anyway? In such a high altitude of 65,000 feet or thereabouts? Wally?''

(41) Wally: ''Well, I think he might have been lookin', well, you know they've got these cameras with these telephoto lenses. Well, he could have just been taking pictures on how they operate things and stuff like that.''

(42) Teacher: ''All right, now this is a good point. Trying to discover Russian operations.''

(43) Steve: ''Another reason for sending that plane over might be they wanted to test the effectiveness of the Russian defenses to see how much chance they

had to go through there."

(44) Teacher: "Now class, what do you think of that? Testing the Russian defenses with an American's life."

(45) Susan: "Well, I don't think it was right because I think he knew that there would be trouble if they did see him and it would just cause trouble for the whole United States."

(46) Teacher: "Sharon."

(47) Sharon: "Well, right at this time there are many other countries in the world that have got, that have come to distrust the United States and with that information that the Russians are giving, saying that we're sending planes over there to spy on them, they could turn the whole world against us."

(48) Teacher: "All right, now this introduces something else, too. We have always prided ourselves on the leadership in the world. Now is this a very good example of leadership? This whole incident, all the facts now that we have? What about the leadership of the United States? Wally?"

(49) Wally: "Well, I don't think something like that shows very good leadership. I mean sending some guys over there and having them check things and see how they're going. A leader, he, he's up there and he's not going to care so much about how they're coming along or something like."

(50) Teacher: "All right, now we have heard several points of view on this problem of the American flyer who was shot down. I think that we could summarize these on the board. Marcia, would you please go to the board and as the things are mentioned, would you write them down and be our recorder in this discussion? Now again, Robert, what were the most important things in this particular incident?"

(51) Robert: "Well, one was should he have been in there, and how did he get, get around to going that way."

(52) Teacher: "All right, now let's put this in a briefer question. Let's state it this way. Why was he there? Karen? Another reason."

(53) Karen: "Well, who sent the man?"

(54) Teacher: "All right, who? I think we could just write down the word who. And we'll remember what this means. Sharon, the next point."

(55) Sharon: "Advantages or disadvantages or . . ."

(56) Teacher: "In other words, why was it done? I think we have that included in why was he there and."

(57) Sharon: "What I meant was what could happen because of this?"

(58) Teacher: "All right, what could happen? That could perhaps be the third point that Marcia could write down. Karen?"

(59) Karen: "Well, we haven't discussed this yet, but, what they plan on doing with the man."

(60) Teacher: "All right, now this is the one point of the discussion we haven't touched on at all. What is going to be the result of this particular incident? Marcia will just write down the word result. All right, with these four things on the board, we certainly don't have the full picture of this incident as yet.

However, it certainly will be developed in the newspapers and in the magazines during the next few days, especially over the weekend now. Over the weekend I would want you to do this: First of all, today we'll just copy down these four little phrases and follow this incident over the weekend. Especially in the Sunday paper there should be a very complete article *(noise in the background)*. Now just a minute! Let's keep our pens and papers and books away 'til I finish giving the assignment. I want you to follow up the incident, get many of the facts and then first of all perhaps a paragraph or two on these four points, and the most important part of the assignment will be this: what do you think the world opinion of the United States is going to be after the full facts have been known? In other words, will our position be a little bit stronger as a world leader or will we be not so strong as a result of this one particular incident? Now are there any questions on this assignment? Karen?"

(61) Karen: "When will this be due?"

(62) Teacher: "This will be due on Monday, this will give you a full weekend to work on this particular assignment. Wally?"

(63) Wally: "What happens if you're to be gone over the weekend?"

(64) Teacher: "Now, of course, you're going to be somewhere where you're going to get a Sunday paper. Be sure now that this type of assignment, remember, that it is done in ink. Pencil is not acceptable in this. Jerry?"

(65) Jerry: "How do we know these newspaper stories are true? Awhile ago when the incident was first discovered they released a statement saying about oxygen shortage or something like that."

(66) Teacher: "Well, now this is one thing that we will perhaps have to judge, all of these different facts now that have been revealed. Certainly in the first set of facts, the United States officials said one thing and the day after that they reversed themselves, so we'll just have to take the facts as they develop and try to determine which is right. And I think now that on Sunday we'll have a full summary article because the Sunday paper is usually very good for this. Sharon?"

(67) Sharon: "Besides doing this, could you get some people's opinion to add on to the end?"

(68) Teacher: "You certainly could do this. Perhaps your parents, especially your fathers who have participated in World War II, might have some opinions on a very important incident like this."

Questions

1. What was the principal source the teacher suggested the students use for obtaining data about this incident?

2. Generally, does the teacher treat this material as a source of reliable facts or of tentative information? (Cite numbers of responses to support your opinion.)

3. Describe your reactions to comments 47, 48, and 49.

FACT OR FANTASY?

4. Describe your reactions to comments 50 through 60.

5. At this point in your understanding of data sources, might you have conducted this discussion differently from the way this teacher did? If so, describe briefly how you might have proceeded.

ACTIVITIES: LABORATORY EXPERIENCE

This is the concluding activity for this chapter. You are asked to design a lesson, present it to a group of students, and conduct a final analysis of your teaching. Procedures for this activity are as follows:

1. Design the lesson according to the following prescribed format.

2. If appropriate, present the lesson to colleagues and refine it before presenting it to students.

3. Conduct and tape-record the laboratory experience with students.

4. Analyze the tape-recordings to assess and refine your instructional effectiveness.

The lesson you will be conducting is essentially the same as the interpreting lesson in Chapter 4. The significant differences are the following:

1. Select a content focus as close to the real world as possible. Therefore, fiction, fantasy, and totally unverifiable topics (for example, will Mars attack Earth?) are not appropriate.

2. Plan the lesson using a prescribed format that requires more precise planning processes than those of the previous lesson.

3. The *main* teaching emphasis in this lesson is on the skill of avoiding judging students' explanations in favor of asking questions that require students to test their own ideas.

Directions

Use the worksheet (pages 129–130) to design an instructional plan according to the format and criteria prescribed below:

1. *Content focus.* Select and state a content focus for presentation and interpretation that meets the following criteria:
   a. An *event* described precisely in relation to time, space, conditions, actions, or interactions; or a *generalization* that explains the cause-and-effect relationship between concepts being considered. For example: *event*—"The presently unresolved issue of whether the oil pipeline

across the tundra of Alaska will do more economic harm than good for the human residents of Alaska.'' *Generalization*—''The construction of the oil pipeline in Alaska is having a major affect on the lives of Alaskan residents.''

    b.   An *event* or *generalization* that is appropriate for the age level. (The event or generalization deals with concepts one would expect the students to have had some previous awareness of and therefore some basic understanding on which to build.)

    c.   An *event* or *generalization* as close to the real world as possible. This criterion may be somewhat difficult to apply because suitable materials for your grade level may not be readily available to you. Science activities are the easiest to employ. However, current events, films, personal experience, and value clarification topics are appropriate. Fiction and fantasy are *not* appropriate for this lesson.

2.   *Objective.* State an objective for the lesson that includes indicators of expected student performance. For example: Students will *describe* previous conditions in Alaska, *explain* the apparent affect of the pipeline on those conditions, and *predict* possible future consequences. All students will demonstrate interest in the discussion by actively participating or actively listening.

3.   *Introductory activity.* Design an introduction to the lesson that presents the event to be considered in as exciting and stimulating a manner as possible. The task is to set the purpose of the lesson and motivate students to become actively involved.

4.   *Development.* Indicate the data source and describe in sequential steps the procedure you will use to involve students in generating and testing ideas. Generally, the development process follows the introductory activity and involves:

    a.   Presenting the data (read article, view film, or observe experiment, and so on)

    b.   Conducting an *interpreting* question sequence using the following types of questions:

        (1)   Open describing

        (2)   Closed describing

        (3)   Explaining

        (4)   Testing questions (explaining, predicting, choosing). The *testing questions* are designed on the basis of what you anticipate the responses will be to the *explaining* questions. For example, suppose you ask the explaining question: ''Why does the water in this container appear clear, while the water in the other appears to contain a considerable amount of sediment?'' Because of the demonstration the students have just observed, you can an-

ticipate that the response will be something like: "Grass keeps water from becoming muddy," or "A ground cover, like grass, prevents erosion from occurring." Therefore, you can design testing questions in advance that deal with anticipated responses: "How do you account for Ashland's drinking water being clear when it comes to us from mountain lakes?" *(Explaining.)* "On the basis of that idea, would you predict that grass is the only thing that we can use to keep running water clear?" *(Predicting.)* If appropriate, you might wish to ask a student to indicate her or his choice between two or more alternatives, placing the student in a position of considering the value* of the idea and the commitment she or he has to that idea. For example, "Supposing that our water could be made purer by additional filtering equipment, would you be willing to pay higher taxes to help purchase the equipment?" *(Choosing.)*

When you conduct the lesson, keep in mind that students are quite likely to state *explanations* at any point in the discussion—not just when you ask explaining questions. Be prepared to employ the testing process whenever explanations are offered. In order to do this, you should be tuned in and listening very carefully to what the students are saying. When an explanation is given, respond by asking a question that calls for the student to test his or her idea. Of course, such flexible and responsive behavior requires practice. You will probably not be very skillful at it the first time you try, but it is like writing behavioral objectives—the first one is tough, but after writing a few million, it's no problem at all!

Before conducting your lesson, you may find it helpful to again read "Procedure for Laboratory Experiences" and "Directions for Taping a Lesson," pages 66–68.

After your lesson, complete the Analysis and Summary: Level of Success sheets, which follow. (If you have been using someone else's classroom, it is a courtesy to send a thank-you note.)

Worksheet: Instructional Plan

1.   Event or generalization: _____

_____

_____

_____

---

*   Remember, a value clarification discussion is appropriate for this laboratory experience. You might wish to consider content that focuses specifically on a value conflict issue. If so, at the ex*plaining* level, you will want to draw out as many alternative ways of coping with a value issue as possible. Testing then becomes a process of asking for *predictions* of possible consequences and *choosing* between alternatives.

2. Objective: _____

    _____

    _____

    _____

3. Introductory activity: _____

    _____

    _____

    _____

4. Development: _____

    _____

    _____

    _____

ACTIVITIES: ANALYSIS OF LABORATORY EXPERIENCE

Directions

As soon as possible after completion of your lab experience, use the following Data Collection Guide to record the information requested below. Be certain to record interactions exactly as they occurred—not as you *intended* them to occur. Play your tape as many times as necessary to accurately record the required data.

1. *Introductory activity.* Record the interactions that occurred during the introduction and indicate any significant variation between what occurred and what was intended.

2. *Development of lesson.*
    a. Record in sequence the questions you asked and the first student response to each question. Code each question according to the *intended* type.
    b. Record any instances of the following in the *teacher* column. Record them as they occur in the discussion sequence and identify each with a brief label: highly judgmental statements (J), psychologically supporting statements (S), psychologically rejecting statements (R), questions or paraphrases to determine personal meaning (PM), and tests of explanations (TE, TP, or TC), for example: "As a result of that idea, how do you account for (explain) . . . ?" (TE). "Would you predict that . . . ?" (TP)

"Would you rather choose . . . ?" (TC).

    c.   Record in the *student* column any student statement or behavior you feel is significant in relation to the outcome of the lesson.

3.   Complete the Summary: Level of Success worksheet and be prepared to share yours with other group members.

Data Collection Guide for Laboratory Experience

Name _____ Date _____

Classroom Teacher's Name _____ School_____

Grade Level _____ Number of Students _____

Teacher	Students

Summary: Level of Success

For each of the categories below indicate your assessment of level of success. Record the student behavior that supports your assessment. Comment on areas you need to improve.

1. *Introductory activity:* _____

    _____

    _____

    _____

    _____

2. *Accuracy of questions.* Fill in the chart below to assess how closely the questions you asked illustrated your intended language action.

Type of Question	No. of Questions Asked	% Accurate
Open describing		
Closed describing		
Explaining		
Predicting		
Choosing		

    Comments:

3. *Seeking personal meaning.* When students used inferential or judgmental words, an attempt was made to determine personal meaning. (Write below the word or phrase for which personal meaning was sought and indicate the technique used to determine meaning.)

4. *Psychological support.* Psychologically supporting statements were supplied and psychologically rejecting statements were avoided. (Write supporting and/or rejecting statements in the appropriate columns.)

Supporting	Rejecting

Comments:

5. *Judging statements.* The judging of students' ideas using highly judgmental terms was avoided. (Write below any highly judgmental terms you used in the lesson.)

    Comments:

6. *Asking students to test their own ideas.* The strategy of asking students to test the validity and/or reliability of their expressed ideas was effectively and successfully implemented. (Review your Data Collection Guide again, and indicate those instances when you did ask testing questions, and those instances when you perhaps should have but didn't.)

    Comments:

7. *Personal reaction.* Summarize your personal reaction to the lesson.

Source Notes

1. Wendell Johnson, *People in Quandaries* (New York: Harper, 1946), pp. 93–99.

2. Neil Postman and Charles Weingartner, *Teaching as a Subversive Activity* (New York: Delacorte Press, 1969), pp. 2–3.

3. Ibid.

4. Ibid., p. 14.

5. S. I. Hayakawa, *Language in Thought and Action* (New York: Harcourt, Brace, 1949), p. 32.

6. William A. Nesbitt, *Interpreting the Newspaper in the Classroom* (Foreign Policy Association, 1971), p. 25.

7. Edwin Fenton, *The New Social Studies in Secondary Schools* (New York: Holt, Rinehart and Winston, 1966), p. 150.

6 *Designing Curriculum for Inquiry Teaching*

Overview*

Rationale

The inquiry process of generating and testing knowledge can, and should, occur naturally and spontaneously many times each day in the ordinary course of events in a classroom. However, it is also the teacher's responsibility to design and present a *planned* program of studies. Often the content of such a program is set forth in a series of course outlines, textbooks, and manuals prescribed by the district. If inquiry is to be an important and integral part of each student's experience in school, then it must also be part of the *planned* program, as well as occurring spontaneously.

General Objectives

At the conclusion of this chapter, you should be able to design a curriculum sequence with the following components:

- The major content goal is identified and stated as a generalization that summarizes the relationships between concepts to be developed.

- A graphic model of the generalization is constructed to illustrate the relationships between concepts to be developed.

- An introductory activity is designed to set the purpose of the instructional sequence and motivate students to become actively involved.

- A series of learning activities is specified that sequentially and developmentally builds appropriate and necessary knowledge, skills, and attitudes to achieve specified cognitive, affective, and psychomotor objectives.

---

* Portions of this chapter may seem to be somewhat redundant. Ideas are presented again which have been emphasized in other chapters. However, in addition to summarizing important ideas, this unit is designed in a manner that permits it to be used independently of the others. It is best used as the final chapter in the series. However, it can also "stand alone" as an independent model of curriculum design and development.

A Curriculum Design Model for Inquiry Teaching*

A number of instructional programs have been developed in recent years that utilize inquiry as a basic learning process.[1] Such programs are often accompanied by detailed manuals and materials presenting the instructional procedures in a detailed and precisely sequenced manner. However, most teachers still face the responsibility of designing their own instructional programs, whose content is often specified in district-adopted textbooks, manuals, and supplementary materials. Inquiry teaching requires the teacher to be able to facilitate students' acquiring data, translating it, organizing it into conceptual categories, and finally interpreting it to generate and test explanations of cause and effect. Unless the teacher is knowledgeable about and skilled in utilizing a curriculum design process that promotes this process, it is very easy to resort to simply "following the textbook."

The curriculum development model presented here is designed to provide the understandings and skills to design lessons and instructional units that facilitate the inquiry process. Once the theory that supports it is understood, and the planning steps have been mastered, the model can be quickly and easily applied to designing single lessons or long-range instructional sequences. The model has proven to be effective for planning instruction at all levels and in all subject matter areas.

Structure of Knowledge

If it is agreed that education is more than the mere acquisition of information — that an educated person is one who is capable of engaging in the process of rational and logical problem solving and decision making, then individuals must be knowledgeable about and skillful in dealing with the semantic structure of language. There are at least three basic reasons why this is so:

1. An essential element in the process of rational decision making or problem solving is the ability to deal constructively with the ambiguity of language. Effective communication takes place when we are able to give or receive mutually understandable and meaningful information. When we give or receive ambiguous, inferential, judgmental, or unverifiable information, communication is ineffective. A basic skill in the knowledge-generating and testing process is being able to recognize and deal with this ambiguity in language symbols.

2. It is a necessity to recognize the tentative nature of knowledge. Much of the subject matter presented to students is either by inference or direct statement presented as factual in nature. In other words, students are led to believe that the content they are considering either did, in fact, exist in the past, or does, in fact, exist now as reported. Such a process denies the manner in which ideas

---

*   Several elements of this model were originally presented in John A. McCollum and Rose Marie Davis, *The Development of Higher Level Thinking Abilities* (Portland, Oreg.: Northwest Regional Educational Laboratory, 1972).

are communicated from one person to another. Any source of data, other than the direct, personal observation of the event or phenomenon being considered, is simply an interpretation of what happened or is happening. If students are to effectively engage in the process of generating and testing their own ideas of the world, they must be aware of the extent to which the data they are using represents the actual world or simply someone's interpretation of the world as seen through the interpreter's personal set of values, cultural patterns, language limitations, and biases.

3. The process of generating and testing ideas requires the ability to find logical, descriptive, and verifiable relationships among sets of objects, events, and/or persons. Learning language is not simply a matter of learning words—it involves correctly relating words to the things and happenings for which they stand. When we call a number of creatures that obviously differ in size, shape, appearance, and behavior, by the same name, *dog*, for example, our nervous system has conceptualized or generalized what is common to them all.

This conceptualizing and generalizing process in language and knowledge development is the basis for understanding and functioning effectively in the knowledge-generating and testing process. The curriculum design model presented here emphasizes three hierarchical levels of knowledge in this process of conceptualizing and generalizing: specific data, concepts, and generalizations (see Chart 6-1).

Specific Data This curriculum design model emphasizes the importance of the learner acquiring items of specific information at the lowest available level of abstraction and as close as possible to the real-world level of direct, personal observation and measurement of the object, event, or phenomenon being considered. Obviously, in order to generate solutions to problems and explain events, one must have information. Data must be available before it can be intellectually processed, and this model emphasizes the acquisition of information as close to the scientifically verifiable report level as is possible to obtain. On this foundation of specific data the knowledge-generating and testing process takes place.

Concepts The next higher level is that of concepts. Concepts are words or phrases that designate categories that represent bodies or sets of specific data obtained through past intellectual and personal experiences: transportation, communication, democracy, communism, environment, culture, community, and on, ad infinitum. Concepts, like any verbal symbol, are obtained and refined through a continual process of discrimination and organization of events. The small toddler standing on the street corner with his father, learning to discriminate between the symbols "car" and "truck," is an example of this process. Billy was involved in his first set of discriminating experiences in the process of developing his concept of transportation. In this initial experience, the elements of cars and truck were organized on a descriptional basis, that is, things with wheels that move. Eventually, however, they

CHART 6-1

3. Generalizations

(Explanations,
inferences, theories)

Statements of cause-effect
relationships between concepts,
usually qualified by degree of
probability. For example:
How people live is affected by
their environment.

2. Concepts

A word or phrase denoting a
category of specific data. For
example: environment (more
inclusive); rainfall, temperature,
topography (less inclusive).

1. Specific Data

Items of specific information as
close to the level of direct observation and measurement as possible.
For example: The average temperature on Guam is 81°, varying annu-
ally between 70° and 90°

would be organized on a much more functional or abstract bases, land vehicles, water vehicles, vehicles powered by an internal combustion engine, and so on. The term *transportation* might be used effectively and logically early in a child's life, but the process of discrimination and refinement continues as long as knowledge about vehicles is discovered and experienced. As concepts are developed they become increasingly abstract and inclusive as more events or elements are added and accommodated to the total. For example, when I describe something round, approximately the size of a baseball or softball, with an orange-colored covering that can be peeled and removed, leaving something that can be divided into sections that contain a tangy juice, what am I describing?

You say, "An orange." All right, now write words in the blank spaces that might categorize each of the following groups:

_____ 1. An orange and an apple

_____ 2. An orange, an apple, and a potato

_____ 3. An orange, an apple, a potato, and water

In each case, I am sure that you found that adding a new element resulted in considerably more abstract and inclusive categories.

Another factor that needs to be recognized in the process of language development is that whatever concept is uttered by an individual, the basis of that concept is unique to that individual. The concept is based on the unique set of discriminating experiences that person has had. It cannot be assumed that my concept of democracy is the same as your concept of democracy, since my discrimination, organization, and refinement of events leading to my formation of this concept are unique to me and different from yours. Consequently, understanding the basis of concept formation is an extremely important element in the communication process, and, most assuredly, understanding and skillfulness in the process of helping students develop concepts is an extremely important element in the teacher's repertoire of teaching strategies. In summary, concepts:

1. Can usually be stated as a word or a phrase with noun quality representing a category of specific information.

2. Are obtained by discrimination and combining of elements or events.

3. Become more abstract and inclusive as more elements or events are added.

4. Have meanings unique to the person expressing them.

Generalizations or Explanations   Finally, in this hierarchy of knowledge, we come to the level of generalizations. The meaning given here to the term generalization is: A statement of cause-and-effect relationships among concepts, usually qualified by degree of probability. For example, in the generalization, "Industry within an area is largely dependent on the availability of raw materials, transportation, and market," we can recognize the concepts "area," "industry," "raw materials," "transportation," and "market." The qualifying word *largely* represents the degree of probability. Many modern curriculum guides and textbooks present generalizations as the knowledge objectives. They may be called "basic ideas," "understanding," or even "concepts." In this program the terms *explanation, in-*

ference, hypothesis, and *theory* have been used interchangeably. All these, of course, indicate *generalizations.*

For example, consider the following statements: "Members of a family have both responsibilities and privileges." "As the size of the community changes, the need for services usually changes." "The amount of heat, light, and water present affects the growth of living plants." "The area of a triangle is one-half the length of the base times the height." "Measures regarded as radical in one generation are often considered moderate in the next." Each presents cause-and-effect relationships between concepts, usually qualified by a degree of probability.*

The exercises that follow provide experience in the identification of this structure of knowledge.

EXERCISES: CLASSIFICATION OF KNOWLEDGE

Directions:

The following language statements have been selected from a specific body of information. Examine each and classify it as:

D—Specific data

C—Concept

G—Generalization

_____ 1.   In 1959, Ohio produced 29,000,000 bushels of wheat.

_____ 2.   Culture.

_____ 3.   Topography.

_____ 4.   The differences in America's topography, natural resources, and population contribute greatly to its industrial economy.

_____ 5.   In 1965, the fish catch in Alaska amounted to 492,614,000 pounds.

_____ 6.   In 1960, there were 1,255,812 foreign-born Italians in the United States.

Answers and Explanations

___D___ 1.   This is a specific data statement verifiable by official report.

---

*   It should be indicated that some people disagree with the thesis that the generalization level of knowledge is higher than the conceptual level. And, indeed, most knowledge can be subsumed under large, abstract conceptual categories. However, the point here is not which is the higher level, but that within generalizations one finds concepts, and the interrelationship of these provides a relatively simple and convenient structure for developing an inductively organized learning sequence.

    C   2. The term culture is a global conceptual category, very abstract and ambiguous, inclusive of much specific data.

    C   3. The term topography, while more denotative of commonly recognized referents, is still an abstract and ambiguous concept.

    G   4. This is a language statement that definitely fits the definition of a generalization: A statement of cause-and-effect relationship between concepts.

    D   5. A data report. Not scientifically verifiable, but undoubtedly verifiable by report.

    D   6. Also a specific data report that can be verified.

Directions

Again, identify each of the following language statements by classifying it as either:

D—Specific data

C—Concept

G—Generalization

        1. Social organization.

        2. Cultural patterns are affected a great deal by environmental conditions and level of technology.

        3. The average American child watches 40 to 50 hours of television each week.

        4. Technology.

        5. Communication media.

        6. Annual rainfall and snowfall in interior Alaska totals less than four inches.

Answers and Explanations

    C   1. A very abstract, ambiguous concept.

    G   2. Very obviously a statement of cause-and-effect relationship between concepts.

    D   3. A verifiable data report.

    C   4. Abstract term. Clearly a concept.

    C   5. Another abstract term or concept.

    D   6. A data report, verifiable by a statistical report.

ACTIVITY: A STRUCTURE OF KNOWLEDGE

Directions

Write a *generalization* from any body of knowledge you want to choose, list the *concepts* evident within that generalization, and state two or three verifiable *data* reports that support one or more of the concepts.

Be prepared to share your responses at the next group session, which will discuss and attempt to reach agreement on the classification of each language statement.

Selecting Generalizations

Many new curriculum guides and textbooks present generalizations that serve as the focal point of the subject matter. These have usually been carefully selected by authorities in the discipline as representing the basic underlying ideas in a particular academic area. However, many curriculum guides and texts still do not do this, and for many, perhaps most, teachers the curriculum development task starts when the available materials are examined to identify those generalizations they consider to represent the basic ideas to be presented. Generally, the content required to be taught at a particular grade level is presented in a basic text or a series of texts. It is the teacher's responsibility to identify and select those ideas that are *worthy* of being taught and to organize them in a logical and teachable manner. However, without having had educational experiences that build the understanding and skill to select and sequence a structure of knowledge, it is very easy to fall into the pattern of simply following the textbook, asking students to proceed page by page, without ever giving serious consideration to how close the information represents reality.

Identifying, selecting, and sequencing a teachable structure of knowledge is not difficult. The task involves:

1. Reading the material.

2. Identifying the major concepts.

3. Developing the main idea or generalization that summarizes the content to be covered.

The following is an example of a brief content statement, concepts included within the statement, and possible teachable generalizations representing basic ideas of the statement:

1. *Content statement.* "Since the discovery and settlement of the New World, great changes are taking place today. With rapidly increasing population, the Latin American countries are striving to make better use of their natural resources in order to improve the living conditions of their people. Like many

other countries, our neighbors to the south have become involved in the struggle between democracy and communism. Today, more than ever, Latin America is playing a vital role not only in inter-American but also world affairs."

2. *Concepts.*
    a. Change: population, natural resources, living conditions.
    b. Interdependence: democracy vs. communism, inter-American affairs, world affairs.

3. *Possible generalizations for teaching focus.*
    a. Latin America is attempting to make better use of natural resources to solve problems of population and living conditions.
    b. Latin America is involved in a struggle between communism and democracy in its role of relating to world powers.

The following activities are designed to give you practice in selecting teachable generalizations for an inductively organized curriculum sequence.

ACTIVITY: ANALYSIS OF GENERALIZATIONS

Directions

Analyze the three generalizations below. Select the one you feel would be the most teachable as a content focus for a specific instructional unit. Indicate opposite each generalization why you feel it is teachable, or why you feel it is not appropriate as a content focus for an instructional sequence. Be prepared to share your judgments at the next group session.

Generalization	Characteristics
1. The steel industry depends on the availablity of coal.	
2. Industry within an area is largely dependent on the availability of raw materials, transportation, and market.	
3. The strength of the United States is its diversity.	

EXERCISE: SELECTING "TEACHABLE" GENERALIZATIONS

Directions

Examine the generalizations below and:

1. Place a plus sign (+) before those you consider to be worthy and teachable generalizations.

2. A minus sign (–) before those you consider not worthy or teachable.

3. A question mark (?) before those you are not sure about.

4. Write a brief statement of the reason for your choice on the line below each generalization.

Be prepared to share and justify your judgments at the next group session.

_____ 1. The police officer is our friend.

_____

_____ 2. The physical environment of an area largely determines the life forms within the area.

_____

_____ 3. Southwest Indians acquired most of their food from the land.

_____

_____ 4. As the size of a community changes, the services within the community often change.

_____

_____ 5. The mountain goat's hoof is uniquely constructed to fit its physical environment.

_____

_____ 6. The cultural patterns of the Colonies were largely determined by the physical environment and cultural patterns brought from the Old World.

_____

_____ 7. The novel often reflects the social issues of the times.

_____

ACTIVITY: FORMULATING "TEACHABLE" GENERALIZATIONS

Directions

1. Read the content below.

2. Formulate one or more generalizations you feel are worthy and teachable.

3. Write your generalizations and a brief statement of rationale for your choice in the space provided at the end of the material. Be prepared to share your responses at the next group session.

Monsoon Asia[2]

Half of the people of the world live in southern and eastern Asia. Why do so many people live there? How do they make a living? What part do they play in world affairs?

You have probably studied several parts of Asia. You may have read about Southwest Asia, for example, the historic lands of the "Middle East." Or you may have read of Siberia and of the Soviet lands in central Asia. But to most of us, the word Asia brings to mind neither Southwest Asia nor Soviet Asia but countries like Japan, China, and India. It means Tokyo, Shanghai, Singapore, Bombay, and other such cities. To most people, Asia means primarily southern and eastern Asia.

We call southern and eastern Asia Monsoon Asia because of one of its important climatic features—the seasonal shifts of wind called monsoons. There are some objections to this term, as you will soon see, but we need a short name for the region. "Southern and eastern Asia" is too long to use repeatedly.

Monsoon Asia is a varied region. Its climate is not uniform. Some parts, like Malaya and Indonesia, are equatorial. Others, like Mongolia, have long, hard winters. Some parts are very wet while others are arid. In peoples and cultures, Monsoon Asia is varied, too. There is no "Asian race" or "Asian culture." People, language, religion, and way of life differ not only from one part of Monsoon Asia to another but even from one part of a country to another.

Yet Monsoon Asia does have unity. Here is a very large and immensely populous region that lies south and east of the great, dry heart of Asia and faces the Indian and Pacific oceans. It has had great and ancient centers of civilization and power, of which India and China have been the best known.

In modern times the civilizations of Monsoon Asia have lagged behind Europe and the United States in economic progress. Now we are seeing great changes in these ancient lands. Old and new ways are meeting and mingling. The problems are difficult. Most of the people are poor and millions are undernourished. Populations continue to grow. Politically there is uncertainty. Dictatorship and democracy and communism and private enterprise contest for these countries. But there are exciting opportunities as well as great problems. When half of the people of the world are in the process of change, the rest of the world had better watch what is happening. Once Monsoon Asia may have been "the languorous East," where time stood still. Today it is very much awake — one of the key areas in world affairs.

Generalizations and Rationale for Choice:

ACTIVITY: FORMULATING A UNIT GENERALIZATION

Directions

Consider carefully a body of subject matter content for which you wish to develop an instructional sequence. Formulate a generalization that:

1. Basically summarizes the ideas you wish the students to acquire.

2. Is teachable.

3. Is worthy of being taught.

Select a topic or area that can be covered in approximately five to ten hours of classroom time. For this activity, avoid subjects that require an extended period of classroom time.

If you have not had previous teaching experience, and/or you are not certain of the subject area you may be teaching, you can obtain the state curriculum guide and select a subject matter area as close to what you may be teaching as now possible to determine.

Generalization:

DESIGNING CURRICULUM FOR INQUIRY TEACHING

GROUP ACTIVITIES: CLASSIFICATION OF KNOWLEDGE

Directions

1. Each participant, in turn, shares the three levels of knowledge formulated and stated for Activity: A Structure of Knowledge, page 142.

2. Each participant, in turn, shares perceptions of the differences in the three generalizations stated in Activity: Analysis of Generalizations, page 143. Discuss perceptions and attempt to agree on which generalization is best for an instructional unit. Following your discussion *(not before),* check your decision with those presented on Response Sheet 1, page 166.

3. Refer to Exercise: Selecting Teachable Generalizations, page 144. Tally on the table below the number of pluses, minuses, and question marks given each generalization.

Generalizations	+	−	?
1.			
2.			
3.			
4.			
5.			
6.			
7.			

    a.   Examine the generalizations that all or most members agree would be worthy and teachable content focuses. What characteristics do they seem to have in common?

    b.   Examine the generalizations that all or most members agree would definitely not be good content focuses. What characteristics do they seem to have in common?

    c.   Examine the generalizations that have two or three question mark tallies. Discuss the reasons for not being sure about them, and attempt to come to a plus or minus decision.

    d.   At this point, develop a set of criteria for selecting a worthy and teachable generalization for instructional unit development. When completed *(but not before),* check your criteria with those on Response Sheet 2, page 167. Discuss similarities and differences. Revise and refine your list until you are comfortable with a set of criteria that fits you.

4. Refer to Activity: Formulating "Teachable" Generalizations, page 145.

    a.   Each participant, in turn, shares generalizations and rationales for choices.

      b.   Using the criteria developed in number 3 or the criteria presented in Response Sheet 2, examine each generalization and discuss the degree to which it fits the criteria.

      c.   Revise, refine, reject, and reformulate until you all feel comfortable in the process of formulating teachable and worthy generalizations.

5.   Refer to Activity: Formulating a Unit Generalization, page 146. Share the generalization you stated as the basic idea around which you planned to design and develop an instructional sequence. Assist each other in stating teachable and worthy generalizations.

Building a Generalization Model

The inquiry, interpreting, knowledge-generating and testing approach to teaching is to help students (1) acquire specific data, (2) organize and classify it logically according to conceptual categories, and (3) perceive and verbalize generalizations (or ideas, explanations, inferences, theories, and hypotheses) logically based on the data. To facilitate this process, it is helpful to construct a model of the generalization that summarizes the content to be taught and that illustrates the relationships among the concepts to be developed.

To illustrate the design process for building a generalization model, let's examine the following *generalization* and identify the concepts within the statement: "Industry within an area is largely dependent on the availability of raw materials, transportation, and market." In order for students to understand this generalization, it will be necessary for them to acquire information to develop the *concepts* of: industry, transportation, market, area, and raw materials.

Let's assume that the generalization has been stated as a knowledge objective for a study of Latin America. In this case, then, area becomes countries in Latin America and/or geographical or political regions within a country. Consequently, we can select specific countries or regions for study that illustrate contrasts in the availability of raw materials, transportation, and market, and thereby illustrate the validity of the generalization.

The structure of knowledge might therefore be arranged as in Chart 6-2. Developing a model such as this gives structure to both the planning and teaching process. The *planning process* is one of moving down the hierarchy of knowledge by:

1.   Identifying the generalization that summarizes the content to be taught,

2.   Identifying the concepts to be developed, and

3.   Determining the specific data needed to develop each concept.

The *teaching process* is one of moving up the hierarchy of knowledge by facilitating students:

1.   Acquiring specific data,

2.   Translating and organizing it according to conceptual categories, and

CHART 6-2

Generalization Model

SUMMARY GENERALIZATION	Industry within an area is largely dependent on the availability of raw materials, transportation, and market.				
CONCEPTS TO DEVELOP	**AREA**	**INDUSTRY**	**RAW MATERIALS**	**TRANSPOR-TATION**	**MARKET**
SPECIFIC DATA TO OBTAIN	Western Venezuela				
	Orinoco Valley				
	Santa Catarina, Brazil				

3. Analyzing data to perceive and verbalize generalizations.

Applying this process of analysis, one can quite simply and quickly develop an illustrative model of most generalizations. Let's use a new *generalization* to illustrate: In primitive societies, culture is influenced significantly by both environment and level of technology. The *concepts* are: primitive societies, culture, environment, and technology.

Generalization Model

PRIMITIVE SOCIETIES	CULTURE				TECH-NOLOGY		ENVIRONMENT		
	FOOD	**CLOTHING**	**SHELTER**	**RELIGION**	**TOOLS**	**CLIMATE**	**TOPOG-RAPHY**	**FLORA**	**FAUNA**
Society 1									
Society 2									
Society 3									

CHART 6-3

In this example the concept of primitive society can be designated by the teacher (or prescribed by the text) as groups of people who live in different areas and exhibit unique social characteristics; for example, woodland, desert, and Plains Indians (Societies 1, 2, and 3 in Chart 6-3). The concept of culture can be broken down into the elements of food, clothing, housing, religion, and so on (each of which, of course, is also a concept), and applied to each of the societies being studied. Technology and environment can be broken down the same way (see Chart 6-3). Other examples of generalization models follow.

Generalization: The physical environment of an area largely determines the life forms in the area. *Concepts:* physical environment, life forms, area (see Chart 6-4).

Generalization Model

CONTRASTING AREAS	LIFE FORMS		PHYSICAL ENVIRONMENT	
	PLANTS	ANIMALS	CLIMATE	TOPOGRAPHY
Northern Alaska				
Oregon				
Arizona				

CHART 6-4

Generalization: Music often reflects the social and economic issues of the period. *Concepts:* music, social issues, economic issues, period (see Chart 6-5).

Generalization Model

PERIODS OF TIME	SELECTIONS OF MUSIC	SOCIAL ISSUES	ECONOMIC ISSUES
16th century			
18th century			
20th century			

CHART 6-5

Once the model is developed, it provides structure for the remaining curriculum design process by: (1) giving a clear indication of what information students will need to acquire in order to develop each concept, (2) indicating what information is *not* necessary to develop an understanding of the concepts to be covered, and (3) showing how the needed information might be organized in order for students to be able to perceive and verbalize cause-and-effect relationships.

Two factors need to be emphasized at this point. First, this generalization model cannot be applied to all statements one considers knowledge objectives. Some objectives may be so ambiguous that it is impossible to develop a table. You will recall that when you analyzed the generalization, "The strength of the United States is its diversity," you found that the concepts strength and diversity were so ambiguous that they were almost indefinable. Even if one broke the concepts down into subconcepts of what might be meant by strength and diversity, the model would be far too cumbersome to be manageable as an instructional sequence. Also, we often find listed as knowledge objectives such statements as "The police officer is our friend." Perhaps a worthy attitude to develop, but hardly a statement that lends itself to the approach being advocated.

Second, this approach has been applied to a single generalization that summarizes the content to be covered. But when one is considering a course of study, it must be possible to apply the model to a *series* of generalizations.

If it were necessary to develop an illustrative model for every single generalization throughout an entire guide, the planning and instructional processes would be far too time-consuming to have utility. For example, in the New York *Social Studies Syllabus* for grade eight,[3] the following generalizations are presented as objectives under the topic "The Colonial Period in the Americas:"

Economic patterns in the major regions of the thirteen colonies were influenced by differences in the physical environment.

Regional economic patterns influenced the development of particular work categories.

Colonial economic patterns were influenced by the economic policies of the mother country.

Although the seaboard English colonies drew population from several European nations in varying proportions, similar cultural patterns developed in most of the colonies.

Generalization Model for a Series of Generalizations

NEW WORLD COLONIES	PHYSICAL CONDITIONS			PATTERNS OF LIVING IN THE OLD WORLD					PATTERNS OF LIVING IN THE NEW WORLD				
	CLIMATE	TOPOGRAPHY	NATURAL RESOURCES	ECONOMY	HOUSING	RELIGION	EDUCATION	GOVERNMENT	ECONOMY	HOUSING	RELIGION	EDUCATION	GOVERNMENT
New England colonies													
Middle colonies													
Southern colonies													

CHART 6-6

Patterns of colonial housing were influenced by geographic factors and by prevailing styles in the mother country.

The differing educational patterns in the colonies developed to some degree because of varied geographic conditions and because of religious attitudes and social structures.

It is apparent that this series of generalizations is related to patterns of living in the Old World as contrasted with patterns of living in the New World. Consequently, an analysis of concepts could result in the model shown in Chart 6-6. An interpretation question sequence can be based on knowledge organized in this manner and would result in student discovery and expression of any of the above generalizations.

The process of designing and constructing models of generalizations may, at this point, appear time-consuming and perhaps even difficult. However, rest assured, it's quickly learned, and when consistently applied to instructional design tasks, it not only provides organizational structure to the knowledge to be taught, but saves a great deal of time in the subsequent task of designing and sequencing learning activities.

Also, the process gives structure to any organized body of data — a speech, a research paper, even a letter to the editor. It answers the questions: "What is the main idea to be presented?" "What concepts need to be developed?" "How do the concepts relate to each other?" It provides a graphic model of the content to be covered and the relationship of ideas.

ACTIVITIES: BUILDING GENERALIZATION MODELS

Directions

1.   On scratch paper, develop models for two or more of the generalizations listed below.

2.   Read pages 148–152 again. Check the models you developed against the criteria presented there. Revise, refine, and redesign until you are satisfied that the models do illustrate the generalizations. Be prepared to share your models at the next group session.

3.   On scratch paper, develop a model of the generalization you formulated to use as the basic idea for an instructional sequence (page 146). Revise and refine until you are satisfied that it accurately illustrates the structure of knowledge to be acquired. Be prepared to describe and justify its structure at the next group session.

Generalizations

1.   Members of a family have both responsibilities and privileges.

2. As the size of a community changes, the services within the community change.

3. The Cold War is essentially the result of two conflicting points of view toward the postwar world, that of the United States and that of the Soviet Union.

4. Measures regarded as radical in one generation are often considered moderate in the next.

5. The novel often reflects the social issues of the times.

6. The short story usually depicts life as a continuous struggle against a hostile world.

7. The structure of an animal is related to its physical environment.

Designing Learning Activities

Once the subject matter content has been analyzed, a summary generalization identified, and a model constructed to illustrate the relationship of concepts to be developed, the task then becomes one of designing and sequencing activities that logically and developmentally build knowledge, skills, and values. Two general questions must be asked at this point:

1. How am I going to *introduce* the sequence?

2. How am I going to involve students in:
    a. *acquiring* data to develop concepts,
    b. *translating* data into meaningful forms and displaying it in a manner that permits relationships to be perceived, and
    c. *interpreting* the data to generate and test explanations of cause and effect?

Chart 6-7 illustrates the general format for planning an instructional sequence that answers these questions.

The Introduction The importance of introducing a new instructional sequence in a manner that sets the purpose and motivates students to become interested and actively involved cannot be overemphasized. The degree to which students see personal meaning in what they are about to study will, to a very large degree, determine whether or not they will learn anything at all. Very small children are generally anxious to please their teacher, and will generally "do as they are told." The elementary school teacher has all kinds of extrinsic motivational devices that can be used with varying degrees of success depending on the group. However, at about the junior high level, when most students begin the process of emancipation from authority, much of the positive reinforcement behavior by teachers is responded to by many students in a manner that clearly indicates that they have come to realize it is a bunch of "crap," an adult put-on designed to control and manipulate. Obviously,

Format for Designing Learning Activities

CHART 6-7

SUMMARY GENERALIZATION

(For example: How people live is affected by environment.)

GENERALIZATION MODEL

Places	Concept 1 (Culture)	Concept 2 (Environment)
Situation 1 (Alaska)		
Situation 2 (Home town)		
Situation 3 (Hawaii)		

INTRODUCTION

An activity that is (1) problem focussed, (2) appropriate for the age and experience of students, and (3) facilitates high interest and involvement.

SPECIFIC OBJECTIVES

Process-oriented objectives; the students will observe, acquire, translate, describe, explain, predict, choose, value, and so on.

LEARNING ACTIVITIES

A series of activities that result in students:

acquiring information as close to the real world as possible,

translating it into a parallel form (maps, graphs, charts, murals, lab reports),

organizing it and displaying it in relation to conceptual categories, and

interpreting it to generate and test explanations of cause and effect.

there are still many students at this level who respond productively to cultural expectations, but the poor secondary school teacher is left with only about two extrinsic motivational devices that have some effect—grades and expulsion from school—and both of these seem to be having less and less of a controlling effect.

It is not the purpose of this text to explore in detail the philosophical and psychological bases for varying methods of teaching.* However, the inquiry process is very clearly based on humanistic ways of *relating* to students rather than behavioristic ways of *controlling* them. That means that the introduction to an inquiry-based instructional sequence—at any level—must set the purpose as a problem *worth* solving, not because the teacher says it's important but because it *is* important, and its importance can be demonstrated. The person designing an instructional sequence must ask: "How can I introduce this lesson (unit) with a problem focus that is reality based and that has *personal* meaning to this group of students, considering their age, their abilities, and their background of experiences?"

Two examples of this type of introduction were given in Chapter 5. One concerned a primary school teacher who began a study of the effect of earthworms on soil and plant growth by simply placing an earthworm on each child's desk with directions to observe its behavior. Another concerned a junior high teacher who introduced a social studies unit on emerging African nations by presenting a vocabulary list of important social, economic, and political terms found in the language of a particular nation with a series of pictures portraying events occurring in that country. The class was organized into small groups with the task, "Come up with as many ideas as you can of what you would expect this country to be like if you had the chance of visiting there next week."

In Chapter 4 an example was given of a science lesson at the secondary level in which students were introduced to the effect of heat on matter by being supplied with bowls of ice, running water, a source of flame, and bimetallic strips at stations throughout the lab. They were given the direction, "With the understanding that we are concerned with heat and matter, see if you can discover relationships or puzzles that you can report back to the class in 30 minutes."

A third-grade teacher began a unit that was focussed on developing the generalization, "People develop organizations to fill their social needs," by giving the class an extra recess period with the following stipulation: "You may not play with anyone else, and you may not talk to anyone else." The subsequent class discussion centered on "What is it like to not have people to talk to?"

A high school teacher began a unit on poetry by asking students to pick a number from 75 to 300. Then, each having paper and pencil, they went outside. The direction was, "Take as many paces, in any direction, as the number you selected. Sit down and record in the next 15 minutes everything you see, smell, hear, taste, feel. Then come back to the classroom." When they returned, the simple structure of a haiku was presented and each student was asked to write one and turn it in, signed or unsigned. The next day the haiku were posted and the discussion of "What is poetry?" began.

---

*   It is suggested that you review "Alternative Bases for Determining Educational Outcomes," Chart 1–1, page 8.

ACTIVITY: DESIGNING AN INTRODUCTION

Directions

Consider the instructional sequence that you are developing. Design an introduction that meets the following criteria:

1. Is problem focussed; for example, the introduction ends with a question such as: "What behavior did you observe?" "Why does it behave that way?" "What would it be like if we didn't have people to talk to?" "What is poetry?"

2. Is appropriate for the group of students you will be working with, considering their age, their abilities, and their background of experiences.

3. Is designed to be personally interesting and worthwhile for the students you will be working with.

    Be prepared to share your introduction at the next group meeting.

Determining Specific Objectives The next step in the process of designing a series of learning experiences is a consideration of *specific* objectives. In addition to the overall knowledge goal, expressed as a summary generalization, specific cognitive, affective, and/or psychomotor objectives need to be identified and stated.

In recent years a great deal has been said concerning the importance of behavioral objectives, systems design models, accountability, and other concepts related to being precise in determining what is to be taught, how it will be taught, and assessing whether or not it has been taught. All of these concepts have been designed to improve the teaching-learning process— and in all likelihood they have. However, this concern for improving educational efficiency has mainly resulted in emphasis on content and has ignored the person and the purpose of the learning process. That is, the focus has mainly been on easily measured subject matters, with seemingly very little attention paid to whether or not it's worth knowing. The point is that the generating of ideas (as opposed to recalling specific information) is a *personal* thing. An idea is right or correct on the basis of its *usefulness,* and that's quite a different measuring problem than simply determining if the student can list certain statements that someone else has made. Consequently, a curriculum design model that has as its focus the inquiry process—the process of students' generating and testing knowledge—must center on the person as well as the subject matter. It must center on *higher cognitive processes* as well as the acquisition of *specific information.* It must center on feelings as well as facts.

Identifying and stating objectives is a different process than that of the teacher's being the sole determiner of what shall be taught and how adequately it has been achieved. In inquiry teaching, the student must be involved in both goal setting and the assessment of achievement. Chart 6-8 illustrates the difference be-

CHART 6-8

TEACHER DETERMINED (Product oriented)	STUDENT INVOLVEMENT (Process oriented)
80% of the class will be able to write a paragraph with four out of five elements evident in correct form.	The class will decide what constitutes an effectively written paragraph. A model will be written on the board and students will judge personal compositions.
Students will be able to state at least three conditions necessary for effective plant growth.	Students will observe plants growing under varying conditions, generate explanations of varying results, and make predictions of future results. In subsequent experiments they will test effectiveness of their predictions.
Students will develop the attitude that fighting is a poor way to solve arguments.	Students will describe various ways people confront conflict. They will generate explanations and make predictions of consequence for each. They will be given the opportunity to express their personal choice, explain their choice, and predict potential personal consequences.

tween teacher-determined behavioral objectives and student involvement in determining behavioral objectives.

Notice that in each of the teacher-determined examples, the objective is product oriented. Emphasis is on the production of a "product" in the form of a *particular* skill, or a *particular* set of ideas, or a *particular* value. In the student involvement examples, emphasis is on the process of learning. The expected outcomes are students involved in deciding, observing, explaining, predicting, testing, and so on. The result sought is the *process* of students actively involved in generating and testing ideas for themselves.

Having said all this about objectives, let me hasten to add that I fully recognize that writing specific objectives is a difficult, time-consuming, and oftentimes frustrating process.[4] A technique I find useful is to begin by generating and sequencing in logical order a series of broadly stated process-oriented goals. For example: "Students will (hopefully) demonstrate enthusiasm, acquire information, translate and display data, generate explanations, test explanations, make and justify choices, and so on."* With this list of desired goals as a guide to identify behaviors to be achieved, the next task is one of identifying, very tentatively, the type of learning activities that might result in the achievement of those goals. The planning format of Chart 6-9 is suggested.

*   Behavioral objective purists—please don't close the book. We'll be coming back to fill in the specific details later.

CHART 6-9

GENERALIZATION

(For example: How people live is affected by environment.)

GENERALIZATION MODEL

Places	Culture	Environment
Ashland, Ore.		
Fairbanks, Ala.		
Agana, Guam		

OBJECTIVES	LEARNING ACTIVITIES
Students will:	
demonstrate enthusiasm	Introduction
acquire information	Identify sources: films, film strips, trip to museum, Mrs. Takauchi, library
translate and display data	Charts, maps (show rainfall, topography, agricultural products); graphs (compare climate); murals of housing and recreation; reports on general life style
interpret data	Question sequence

ACTIVITY: IDENTIFYING TENTATIVE GOALS AND LEARNING ACTIVITIES

Directions

Consider the instructional sequence you are developing. Think of the kinds of behaviors you wish students to be able to perform and generate a tentative list of these behaviors and place them in a sequence that builds developmentally to the final outcome. Despite everything you have learned previously about behavioral objectives, consider such broad and ambiguous terms as: "Students will develop understanding, appreciation, interest, and so on." Also consider such process-oriented behaviors as: "Students will observe, determine, acquire, describe, translate, express, construct, display, interpret, explain, predict, choose, and so on." Opposite each goal, indicate activities that might develop that goal. Try to generate as many ideas as possible. Use whatever sources are available to find ideas. Be creative if possible, but don't hesitate to beg, borrow, steal, and/or plagiarize at this point. Everything is fair in the process of locating ideas that will be interesting, involving, and worthwhile for students.

Be prepared to share your goals and learning activities at the next group meeting.

Acquiring, Translating, and Interpreting Data   The next task is one of designing *specific* learning experiences that result in students (1) acquiring information, (2) translating it into parallel forms, and (3) displaying it in a manner that can be utilized to perceive and express relationships among concepts. Another consideration is that of class organization. Let's consider each of these in greater detail.

Acquiring Data   A basic consideration in the process of selecting materials and identifying procedures is the degree to which it is possible to involve students in real world experiences. There are two very important reasons for this. First, if education is considered to be a process of preparing students to be able to function effectively in the real world of life, then obviously we ought to try to involve them in real-world learning experiences. When this is not possible, we certainly should try to simulate the real world in the classroom. Second, research conducted by Jean Piaget and others has clearly indicated that most elementary school and many secondary school students simply can't learn through highly abstract, symbolic materials. The formal operational stage identified by Piaget, at which time individuals can deal effectively with abstractions, does not *begin* until the individual is functionally 12 years of age, and it takes at least three years for this ability to be fully developed (see Chart 6-10).

Consequently, the question that must be asked at every point in the design and teaching process is: "Where is each student in relation to her or his level of maturity?"

Piaget's Developmental Stages and Adequate Data

DEVELOPMENTAL STAGES	ADEQUATE LEARNING DATA
Preoperational (2–7 years)	Real-world simulations (models, games, role playing, movies)
Concrete operations (7–11 years)	Manipulative materials (concrete objects that represent symbols) Visual materials (maps, graphs, pictures, etc.)
Formal operations (11–15 years)	Symbols (numerals, words, imagination)

CHART 6-10

Given Piaget's research, any attempt to teach principally from a textbook until well within the high school years is simply ridiculous. Any experienced elementary school teacher will tell you, "If you can't take children to a farm, you can forget about their developing a concept of a cow." And yet, in about the third grade, students become the victims of textbooks. Throughout the world, millions of kids are sitting in classrooms right now, looking at written symbols and being told, "That's the real thing."

Directly related to the phenomenon of treating the symbol as though it were the real world is the lack of attention we give to the right hemisphere of the brain, which controls nonlogical, metaphoric, and intuitive capacities. Recent research indicates that our lack of consideration for the right side of the brain has penalized many, perhaps even most, individuals to the point of significant intellectual damage.[5] Utilization of the analytical, logical, symbolic textbook approach as the *only* methodology perpetuates that damaging process. All individuals—*at any age*—need visual and manipulative experiences to develop normally and completely.

Translating Information into a Parallel Form   Since the intellectual process of generating and testing ideas is dependent on perceiving cause-and-effect relationships within a field of data, specific factual information must be obtained and displayed in a manner that provides the opportunity to perceive such relationships. That means, as students acquire information from such sources as: field trips, resource people, films, filmstrips, tape-recordings, records, laboratory experiences, gaming experiences, diaries, magazines, textbooks, and so on, they should be asked to translate the information into a parallel form and present it to the class in a manner that facilitates interpretation. Examples of activities that provide for this translation and presentation process are: building a model, constructing a mural, summarizing data on a chart, building a graph, illustrating a map, producing a film or filmstrip, giving a demonstration, role playing, dramatics, and so on.

This is the level at which *concept development* occurs. Students put together the information they have obtained and literally build a concept—of poetry, folk music, friction, fables, transportation—of whatever concept is being developed. That is, the students acquire, translate, organize, and display information in a manner that facilitates interpreting the data to express explanations of cause-and-effect relationships.

Organizing an Information Display   The process of acquiring factual data, organizing it into conceptual categories, and analyzing it for relationships that can be expressed as generalizations requires that information be organized into a display that provides the opportunity to perceive such relationships. If the factual data students acquire are simply in the form of individual written reports, the perception of relationships within the data is most likely to be highly inhibited, if not totally prevented from occurring. The inquiry process requires that students be able to examine and interpret the total data acquired. Consequently, as information is acquired and expressed, it is essential that it be displayed in a manner that provides this opportunity. There are a number of ways that this can be accomplished.

Primary level: Since primary school children may not have acquired the proficiency in reading to be able to interpret many written forms of expression, information displays at this level must of necessity be organized in the form of illustrative materials. For example, a second-grade class, involved in a study of homes in relation to environment, expressed data in the following forms:

1.   Three cut and paste murals of
     a.   homes in their community (temperate zone),
     b.   homes in a hot, wet environment,
     c.   homes in a hot, dry environment,
     d.   homes in an arctic environment.

2.   Four charts listing the materials available for construction in each environment.

3.   Four charts listing the construction tools and skills utilized in each environment.

4.   A series of drawings illustrating types of homes found in each environment.

5.   A display of building materials found in their own neighborhood.

In a planned discussion which asked the children to examine similarities and differences in the four environmental areas, these second graders verbalized a number of perceived relationships, including the following:

"People use the materials they have to build houses."

"It takes different kinds of workers to build different kinds of houses."

"People build houses according to the kind of weather they live in."

"People build houses to fit their needs."

Intermediate, upper grade, and secondary levels: Since most of these students have proficiency in reading, information displays may be composed of charts, graphs, maps, and illustrations that are largely symbolic and represent the total data researched. Even though the students' research may be in the form of notes or translated into written reports, it is essential that the basic ideas of the information they gather be translated into a form that can be displayed and interpreted by the entire class.

An effective way to organize and display such information is the generalization model we have already discussed. The development of a large display such as Chart 6-11 (readable by students at any location of the room), which presents the basic and essential researched data, facilitates perceiving relationships in the generalizing process.

This is not intended to imply that it is not important to have upper grade and secondary school students express and display information in the form of murals,

Display of Essential Data

CHART 6-11

SOCIETIES	CULTURE					ENVIRONMENT		
	Food	Clothing	Shelter	Gov't	Religion	Climate	Topography	Flora & Fauna
Society 1								
Society 2								
Society 3								

drawings, creative stories, plays, poetry, and other forms of expression. All of these are worthwhile forms of expression at every level. They can and should be incorporated into an information display.

Departmentalized organizational structure: It is obvious that the above suggestions can be most effectively implemented in the "self-contained classroom" where the teacher is responsible for the instruction of only one group of students. The teacher who is faced with the responsibility of instructing several groups of students each day obviously does not have the space available to have each group make and display as many as five information displays.

One technique for dealing with this problem is to have all reports, maps, graphs, reviews, and so on produced in final form on ditto-masters so that enough copies can be reproduced so that all students can have one. An agreed-on format of organization can then be developed so that all students will analyze and interpret the same data.

Another technique that has been used successfully is to have each class construct a large generalization model on butcher paper, which can be rolled up and stored at the close of each period.

Class Organization   How should the class be organized for the most effective acquiring and processing of data? Many teachers (and students) dislike having the class organized into committees for study purposes. In fact, in many traditional committees, one verbal and motivated child usually does all or most of the work. However, when making the decision as to whether committees will be organized or all work will be accomplished by each individual student, it would seem that at least three factors should be considered:

1.   In the American system of democratic decision making and private enterprise, (a) most decisions are made by groups, (b) most ideas, if not a product of groups, are at least developed and refined by groups, and (c) much of the work

of our society is accomplished by groups. The point is—students need experiences of engaging effectively in group processes.

2. Many group products do end up looking like a giraffe when they are supposed to look like a horse, for the simple reason that little, if any, attention is paid to the skills of group interaction. Any committee needs to be structured very carefully, with the teacher initially meeting with the group to assist in making decisions relative to (a) goal identification, (b) material selection, (c) defining specific procedures for goal attainment, and (d) evaluation techniques for assessing progress. However, beyond this, students *can* be taught interpersonal communication skills. Such skills are not the subject of this text, and will not be discussed here; however, it is strongly recommended that teachers acquire interpersonal communication and group process skills themselves, and translate these into experiences for students.

3. The traditional committee activity of giving reports has absolutely no value for the inductively organized curriculum sequence. In the inductively organized instructional sequence, *committees should function for the explicit purpose of researching, translating, and expressing data for the use of the rest of the class.* That is, each committee must consider: (a) what information does the class need, (b) where can we find that information, (c) how can we most efficiently gather the information, and (d) once we have the information, how can we express it in a form which the rest of the class can best utilize (chart, map, graph, illustrations, or a combination of these)? This way, the committee becomes a data source for the entire class, serving a very useful and important function.

Chart 6-12 is a management grid that has proven helpful in organizing a committee and subsequently monitoring its activities. It has been used successfully at both the elementary and secondary levels.

Organization of Committee Work

TASK	TASK FORCE	RESOURCES	PRO-CEDURES	PRODUCTS	COMPLETION DATE
1. Determining agricultural products	Jim, John, Sally	Library, *Brazil* (film), ?	Research, combine notes	Product map, charts, ?	3/8/78
2.					

CHART 6-12

Final Interpreting Activity   After students have acquired information, translated it, organized it into conceptual categories, and presented it in the form of an information display, the final student activity is interpreting the data—the process of generating and testing ideas. Thus the final task in the curriculum design process is specifying an interpretation question sequence that results in students analyzing the data, generating explanations of cause-and-effect relationships, and testing the usefulness of their ideas.

ACTIVITIES: REFINING LEARNING ACTIVITIES

Directions

Return to the set of tentative goals and learning activities you developed in the previous activity. Now, extend and refine each of them. Attempt to be specific in relation to: (1) the behaviors you wish students to perform, and (2) the learning activities that students will experience in the process of achieving those behaviors.

Example

OBJECTIVES	LEARNING ACTIVITIES
Students will: acquire, translate, and organize data to develop the concept of agriculture in Brazil.	1. Research available textbooks. (Review note-taking and outlining skills.) 2. Develop outline of information from the films shown. 3. Construct agricultural products map. 4. Construct chart listing products and indicating annual production.

Put your instructional sequence into final form and be prepared to share it at the next group meeting.

Source Notes

1. Examples of instructional programs utilizing inquiry as the basic teaching-learning process are: AAAS, *Science: A Process Approach (SAPA II)* (Lexington, Mass.: Ginn and Company); BSCS, *Biological Science: An Inquiry into Life* (New York: Harcourt Brace Jovanovich); Holt Data Bank, *Elementary Social Studies* (New York: Holt, Rinehart and Winston); *Man: A Course of Study* (Washington, D.C.: Development Association).

2. Stephen B. Jones and Marion Fisher Murphy, *Geography and World Affairs* (Chicago: Rand-McNally, 1966), p. 304.

3. *Social Studies Syllabus,* grade 7 and grade 8 (Albany, N.Y.: University of the State of New York and the State Department of Education, Bureau of Secondary Curriculum Development, 1965).

4. You might find the following manual helpful when writing objectives with emphasis on student involvement: John A. McCollum, *How to Work Behavioral Objectives and Still Teach Creatively* (Ashland, Oreg.: L.R. Publishers, 1977).

5. The following references provide a comprehensive overview of the theory and research related to the development of the right hemisphere of the brain: Jerome Bruner, *On Knowing: Essays for the Left Hand* (Cambridge, Mass.: Harvard University Press, 1969); Madeline Hunter, "Right-Brained Kids in Left-Brained Schools," *Today's Education* (December, 1976); Robert E. Samples, "Learning with the Whole Brain," *Human Behavior* (February, 1975).

A FINAL COMMENT

It is my sincere hope that you have found this book to be a valuable learning experience. The set of teaching strategies that facilitates students generating and testing ideas for themselves is not the easiest teaching process to conduct. Obviously, it's much easier to ask students to simply read the chapter and answer the questions in the study guide. However, there is evidence to support the belief that the teaching process of dispensing information produces people who are dependent on others for the solution of problems, while the inquiry process produces independent thinking and problem solving. It's clear that the problems students in the schools of today must face as adults of tomorrow demand independent, creative thinking to solve. Hopefully, this program has been helpful in providing you with the necessary understandings and skills to facilitate inquiry occurring as an important and integral part of learning in your classroom.

Response Sheet 1:
Activity: Analysis of Generalizations

1. The steel industry depends on the availability of coal.

1. This generalization is, of course, teachable. However, it is *very* limited in scope as an instructional focus. For one thing, the steel industry depends on a great deal more than just the availability of coal.

2. Industry within an area is largely dependent on the availability of raw materials, transportation, and market.

2. This second generalization clearly fits the definition of a generalization: A statement of cause-and-effect relationships between concepts, qualified by degree of probability. It is specific enough to communicate rather precisely, yet abstract enough to be inclusive of much data. Also, the concepts are all manageable, that is, data should be readily available to develop the concepts of industry, raw materials, transportation, and market. It would seem to be worthy of being taught in that it applies to the economics of any enterprise, large or small business, private or public industry.

3. The strength of the United States is its diversity.

3. The problem with this statement is that it is so abstract and ambiguous that it really doesn't communicate. The concepts of strength and diversity are so ambiguous, so inclusive, that they are almost undefinable and hence unteachable. (By specifying more precisely what is meant by strength and diversity, several teachable generalizations *could* be developed.)

Response Sheet 2:
Criteria for Selecting Teachable Generalizations

1. The generalization contains two or more concepts presented in the form of a cause-and-effect relationship.

2. The generalization typically contains a word or phrase denoting degree of probability (for example, usually, often, generally, largely, and so on).

3. The concepts have meaning (that is, specific data are available for their development).

4. The generalization is worthy of being taught. (It represents basic instructional knowledge of the content area being studied, and it's worth the time and effort both the teacher and students spend in learning about it.)